Disaster Risk Management and Reconstruction in Latin America

Praise for this book

'This is a book to be read and understood before a disaster happens and not afterwards if early responses to reconstruction are not to lead to greater problems.'
  Gustavo Riofrío, Consultant with DESCO (Centro de Estudios y Promoción del Desarrollo), Peru.

Disaster Risk Management and Reconstruction in Latin America
A technical guide

Bárbara Montoro and Pedro Ferradas

With Miguel Muñoz, Douglas Azabache, Orlando Chuquisengo,
Julio Calderón, Luis Rodríguez, Giovana Santillán, Franklin Ocmin,
Bécker Pérez, Dante Muñoz

PRACTICAL ACTION
Publishing

Practical Action Publishing Ltd
The Schumacher Centre,
Bourton on Dunsmore, Rugby,
Warwickshire, CV23 9QZ, UK
www.practicalactionpublishing.org

Spanish edition, 2005
English edition, revised and extended, 2014
Copyright © Practical Action, 2014

ISBN 978-1-85339-672-4

Since 1974, Practical Action Publishing (formerly Intermediate Technology Publications and Practical Action Publishing) has published and disseminated books and information in support of international development work throughout the world. Practical Action Publishing is a trading name of Practical Action Publishing Ltd (Company Reg. No. 1159018), the wholly owned publishing company of Practical Action. Practical Action Publishing trades only in support of its parent charity objectives and any profits are covenanted back to Practical Action (Charity Reg. No. 247257, Group VAT Registration No. 880 9924 76).

Coordination: Doris Mejía and Alejandra Visscher
Cover photo: Practical Action, Peru
Photographs: Practical Action, Bárbara Montoro and Miguel Muñoz
Cover design by Practical Action Publishing
Typeset by Practical Action Publishing
Printed in the United Kingdom

Contents

Acknowledgements

The authors thank the Tony Bullard Trust foundation, for the financial aid provided for research and publishing purposes; German Agro Action and the UNDP, for the assistance provided for the implementation and systematization of Practical Action reconstruction projects; Architect Luis Solari and engineer Gladys Villagarcía, who selflessly provided information and contributed their professional experience; and the professionals of the CEOP ILO consortium, Zenón Coris and Eva Centeno, who contributed their opinions.

Thanks are also due to Miguel Muñoz, Douglas Azabache, Orlando Chuquisengo, Julio Calderón, Luis Rodríguez, Giovana Santillán, Franklin Ocmin, Bécker Pérez, Dante Muñoz who assisted in the writing of this book.

'Without departing from your subject of Lisbon (the earthquake), admit, for example, that nature did not construct twenty thousand houses of six to seven stories there, and that if the inhabitants of that great city had been more equally spread out and more lightly lodged, the damage would have been much less and perhaps of no account.'

Letter from Rousseau to Voltaire dated 18th August 1756.

Preface to the second edition

It is estimated that nearly 90% of the victims of disasters are from developing countries, the reason being that in those countries, the people and their housing are more vulnerable to disaster. Their vulnerability is usually poverty-related, as poor people struggle to gain access to safe housing conditions or safe public and/or private systems to relieve the impact of disasters.

An analysis of the losses caused by disasters would show that although the number of losses is greater in developed countries, the impact disasters cause in developing countries is far more significant when one compares the income of the affected families with the Gross Domestic Product (GDP) of the country in question. It is evident for example, that the loss of a sheep for a poor peasant family is much more 'disastrous' than the loss of 50 heads of cattle for a large cattle farming company. It is estimated that in less developed countries, losses caused by disasters represent a percentage of GDP 20 times higher than the proportion of GDP lost in more developed nations.

In Latin American history, disasters are undoubtedly a determining factor. They have caused about half a million fatalities over the last century and 70,000 over the last decade; millions of casualties, the majority of them humble; and huge economic losses. For example, in the 1972 earthquake in Moquegua, the losses exceeded 100% of the GDP of Nicaragua; and with Hurricane Mitch in 1998, the losses were equivalent to 150% of the GDP of Honduras and Nicaragua combined. In the case of the 1997–1998 El Niño Phenomenon, the losses were equivalent to 14.6% of the GDP of Ecuador, 7% of the GDP of Bolivia and 4.5% of the GDP of Peru.

The destruction of housing and social infrastructure has reached unimaginable levels. In El Salvador, it is estimated that 330,000 homes were destroyed or seriously damaged by the 2001 earthquakes; the floods and mudflows that occurred during the 1997–1998 El Niño Phenomenon in Ecuador, Peru and Bolivia destroyed or damaged 135,000 homes; the earthquake in Mexico in 1985 destroyed about 30,000 buildings and damaged 67,000; the most recent earthquake in Peru (August 2007) destroyed approximately 76,000 homes and damaged more than 30,000.

Existing threats in Latin America are related to the frequent recurrence of destructive phenomena such as earthquakes, volcanic eruptions, cyclones and floods.

It is proof of the scale of seismic activity in the region that three of the world's strongest earthquakes of the last 100 years occurred in Latin America: one in Ecuador in 1906 (magnitude 8.8); one in Argentina in 1922 (8.5); and one in Chile in 1960 (9.5 degrees). This last was one of the strongest earthquakes ever recorded on the planet, although as it occurred in a relatively unpopulated region, it did not cause as much damage as others of less magnitude.

Earthquakes have caused a large number of fatalities in the region during the past 40 years:

31 May 1970, Peru (7.8 degrees): 69,000
23 December 1972, Managua, Nicaragua (6.5): 6,000
4 February 1976, Guatemala City (7.5): 23,000
19 September 1985, Mexico City (8.1): 10,000[1];
1986, San Salvador (7.5): 1,500
2001, San Salvador (two earthquakes: 7.6 and 6.6):1,150
5 March 1987, Quito, Ecuador (7):1000
1994 and 1999, Paez, and the central region of Colombia: 1,938

Some earthquakes are also related to volcanic activities, which are a latent hazard in this content. The eruption of La Soufriere (San Vicente), Pele (Martinique) and Santa Maria (Guatemala) volcanoes in 1902 together caused the death of 43,500 people. In 1982 the eruption of the Chichon volcano in Mexico killed 2,000 people and in 1985 the eruption of the Nevado del Ruiz caused 23,000 fatalities, burying the town of Armero in Colombia. Earthquakes and volcanic eruptions have given rise to tsunamis which destroyed entire coastal towns in countries like Chile, Peru and Nicaragua, as well as alluviums that buried entire towns, as occurred in Peru in 1970.

Lethal cyclones have struck Central America and the Caribbean, particularly Fifi in 1974 (10,000 deaths in Honduras), Liza in 1976 (2,500 victims in Mexico), Davin in 1979 (1,278 fatalities in the Dominican Republic), Mitch in 1998 (12,000 deaths in Central America) and Stan in 2005 (more than 1,500 deaths, mainly in Guatemala).

Other destructive events that occur frequently and have a great impact are the floods and avalanches of mud and rocks that occur every year as a result of heavy rain, which tend to become more intense within the context of the El Niño and La Niña phenomena. Although rain-related floods and alluviums cause fewer deaths than earthquakes, eruptions and cyclones, they nevertheless cause the destruction of thousands of homes; the extreme rainfall in Venezuela in 1999 caused more than 15,000 victims and left 100,000 people homeless as a result of landslides, cave-ins and floods on the hillsides.

The disasters in Latin America are increasingly influenced by mankind and society: on the one hand, deforestation and contamination are on the rise owing to the growing frequency and intensity of climate-related phenomena such as rain, floods and alluviums; on the other hand, the unsuitable location and deficient construction of housing, public services and productive infrastructure make them especially vulnerable to destructive phenomena.

In Latin America, poor, and even middle-class people who frequently have limited opportunities to gain access to the housing market, develop progressive housing construction strategies that entail reciprocal work and solidarity on the part of extended families and friends. These are referred to as self-construction strategies. Self-construction without technical assistance is a misguided solution, as although it has enabled poor people to gain access to housing, such dwellings tend to be highly vulnerable, particularly as many are built on land susceptible to destructive phenomena, using inappropriate construction technologies. The vulnerability of such housing has increased owing to a lack of policies that could influence the mechanisms through which poor people commonly gain access to housing: the occupation of marginal land and construction reliant on traditional neighbourhood or community know-how.

For many years, Latin American countries have responded to disaster situations through humanitarian aid programmes and the restoration and reconstruction of the affected infrastructure and basic services. Where State interventions are concerned, reconstruction experiences have usually involved a planning process from the top, and implementation has delivered unequal results. The State has generally been involved in reconstruction after major disasters, tending to neglect reconstruction linked more localized to disasters of less magnitude and in rural areas.

Housing reconstruction by State institutions usually involves the promotion of loans, enabling victims to gain access to housing built by private companies or government programmes. Interventions whereby affected families build with their own means usually result in precarious, unsafe housing and a proportion of social infrastructure may be delayed several years, seriously lowering the standard of living of the victims.

There are some extreme cases that illustrate this situation. Following the recent earthquake in Peru, peasants simply replaced the adobe bricks in walls that had cracked, thus increasing the vulnerability of their family homes. Another concerns the 'provisional' houses donated by the German cooperation agency after the floods in Chosica (Peru) in 1981, in which the victims of those floods are still living 27 years later.

Although the reconstruction effort conducted by governments and private companies helped solve the problem for one sector of the affected population, it generally related to programmes or projects in which local organizations and institutions were unable to participate, and the need for public areas that respond to the needs and traditions of the population were not taken into account. The tendency of such programmes or projects was to relocate the victims in smaller spaces than they lived in previously, with limited prospects for expansion to respond to the demands of changing activities and growing families in the future. Furthermore, these programmes were often used for political lobbying or electoral purposes, demonstrating a paternalistic approach that relocated people, reduced their self-esteem and cast aside their traditional local 'ayni' and 'minka' systems of organization for joint community work.

Despite the limitations described above, reconstruction from the top apparently offers some advantages, such as the belief that the houses are of a better quality, the fact that they are built quickly without the delays involved when the beneficiaries have to be consulted and reach consensus, and the relative experience and knowledge of construction among formal construction companies when compared to that of beneficiaries.

During the last decade, important innovations have been made in reconstruction, including the development of programmes and projects in which community-based reconstruction is more frequently considered. This change is taking place without undermining the mechanisms promoted by the State to gain access to public and private credit, because it has been proved that an important segment of the victims are unable to take advantage of such mechanisms as they cannot meet the minimum requirements: providing proof of a stable income and documents certifying the ownership of their property. Consequently, the only alternative for this segment is to rebuild their homes with their own resources, without adequate technical guidance nor access to the assistance and/or advice provided by non-governmental organizations (NGOs).

Community-based reconstruction supported by NGOs is upheld by the extensive self-construction practices that many families resort to as the only alternative for rebuilding their homes after a disaster. When such efforts are geared towards the most poverty-stricken people – improving the organization of affected families, bearing in mind the ongoing risk of disasters, and encouraging the participation of local institutions by employing local resources and providing access to technical construction advice – people are able to improve their skills and reduce their housing costs.

The majority of the participatory reconstruction experiences described in this book refer to seismic disasters that have occurred in Peru. Experiences in other countries also need to be analysed in order to build better intervention models. In this respect, the experiences of certain NGOs in El Salvador in which local governments were strongly involved are relevant, as is the recent reconstruction experience following the tsunami in southern Asia, where Practical Action promoted the use of appropriate technologies among the different public and private institutions involved in the reconstruction process.

As proposed in this book, it is necessary to continue improving reconstruction processes in order to ensure adequate local participation, enhance the application of construction techniques, deal with the higher costs incurred when working in more remote and marginalised rural areas and ensure access to housing for the homeless (tenants and occupants of unsuitable land). Undoubtedly, these are all contributions to the efforts to reduce poverty.

Pedro Ferradas, Lima

Note

1. The Mexican government initially reported the number of deaths to be 6–7,000. Years later, however, when additional information emerged from various sources, it was calculated that the death toll was 35,000, although there are sources that claim that the true figure exceeded 40,000.

Introduction

Reconstruction is a far more complex process than designing and building housing, as it involves poverty-stricken families. As poor people cannot gain access to the housing market or to the loans the State grants as a way of responding to the impact of disasters, consideration must be given to self-construction, which has been the main mechanism for poor people to gain access to housing.

Self-construction, the process whereby people build their own homes together with their families or neighbours, is derived from a combination of building procedures that migrants have learnt empirically or orally, in geographical areas that are usually very different from their native habitats and using unconventional materials. The most prominent of these materials are adobe bricks (which poor people prefer because they are more affordable and have thermal qualities; they are, however, less resistant to earthquakes and floods, despite efforts made to make them stronger by adjusting their size, reinforcing their structure or using them in combination with other materials); 'quincha' (traditionally used on the coast and in jungle areas of Peru and considered the most appropriate alternative in the San Martin region in the early nineties); and more recently, cement blocks (manufactured to replace clay bricks, mainly for constructions in urban areas).

Self-construction enables poor families to take advantage of their own resources and skills to gradually build homes that respond to their needs. This is the way the majority of the population have built their homes, although it is usually associated with the occupation of unsuitable land (loose soil prone to sliding and flooding), construction processes that lack technical guidance and insufficient maintenance and protection. Objectively, this means that the construction procedures validated by current international standards are irrelevant to the majority of the population in Peru and that self-construction is usually associated with an increase in risk.

The highest risk constructions are linked to potential fatalities, ill-health and the destruction or deterioration of the habitat or livelihoods of the victims. Families can also be adversely affected by the destruction or loss of their furniture and household appliances, or by their water supply being cut. Children may also suffer as a result of damaged schools. Affected communities associate disasters with the loss of not only their homes, but also community spaces such as their church, school, medical post and community buildings, among others.

Risk has been defined as the possible occurrence of disasters linked to specific hazards or vulnerability factors. Risk levels can be estimated according to the losses and damages that a specific disaster could cause.

Hazards are probable occurrences of potentially destructive events, such as earthquakes. Vulnerability is a complex social process that implies the degree to which people and assets are exposed to hazards, such as the inability or weakness of the population and institutions to anticipate, deal with and recover from the impacts of dangerous events.

Vulnerability is a key concept in understanding disaster risks and, therefore, a key consideration when proposing strategies and reconstruction plans. People, families and institutions build up their vulnerability daily through their decisions and their actions, which are determining factors for the sustainability of their habitat and their livelihoods. Vulnerability depends on numerous physical, environmental, economic, social, political, institutional and organizational factors generated both locally and in larger geographical areas.

Vulnerability is associated with the limited number of people who are able to exercise their rights, their migratory processes, the effects on them of public policies and the lack of security for these people, their habitats and their livelihoods (see Figure 1).

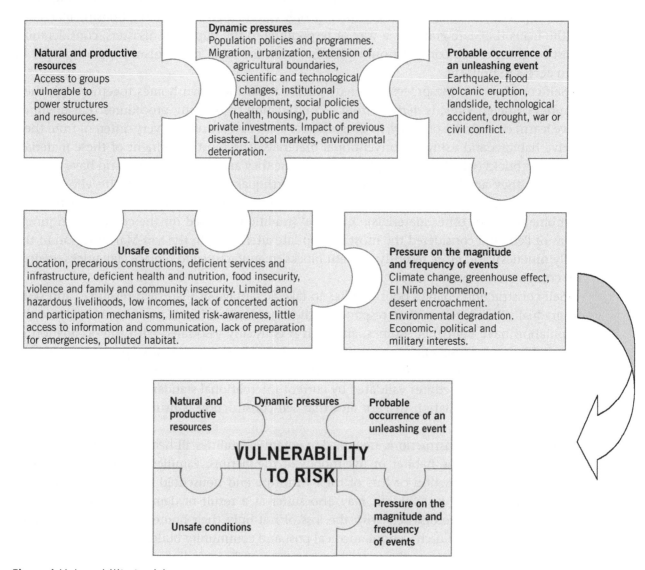

Figure 1 Vulnerability to risk

A concept that is also worth taking into consideration in a reconstruction process is the 'resilience' factor, which implies putting more emphasis on what the communities can do for themselves and how they can reinforce their skills, rather than only concentrating on their vulnerability to the disaster or their needs in an emergency situation. Another equally important idea that should be considered as a complementary approach is the 'livelihoods' concept put forward by DFID (UK Department for International Development), which indicates that livelihoods consist of the skills, assets, resources, opportunities and activities required in order to survive. The variety and quantity of capital a person, a household or a social group possesses can be a factor in determining the speed and effectiveness of the reconstruction process. Livelihoods provide an income or a way of gaining access to resources in order to meet basic needs, for example, farming, livestock-raising, tapping natural resources, tourism, and trade.[1]

If disasters are caused by the hazardous conditions generated during the development process, then the reconstruction process must prevent a repetition of such conditions. A reconstruction project focused solely on the recovery of damaged or destroyed infrastructure would not be sufficient, as it would not eliminate the fundamental causes of the disaster. Reconstruction must be understood to be an opportunity for more sustainable development and for strengthening the skills and livelihoods of the population and of the institutions that carry out activities in the affected areas, aimed at better management of disaster risks.

Consequently, reconstruction should not be narrowly focused on ruined housing and services, but also on investment in infrastructure such as irrigation systems, in the case of farmers, or the facilities in which people carry out their productive or business activities.

Note

1. Livelihoods include five types of capital: human capital (knowledge, skills, health, capabilities, etc.); social capital (social aid systems, political power, participation in formal groups, etc.); natural capital (access to and maintenance of the quality of natural resources essential for survival); physical-material capital (production tools, housing, shelters and road infrastructure, for example, transport, communications, water and sanitation, etc.); and financial capital (availability of cash).

CHAPTER 1

Vulnerability, disaster and housing in Peru

This chapter contains general information on earthquake-related risk and disasters, which is essential background for understanding the approach to housing reconstruction processes described in the following chapters. It contains an account of the earthquakes that have occurred in Peru and outlines the characteristics of the country's cities and towns, architectural designs, traditional building technologies and the construction materials most used by the poor, as well as the poverty-related vulnerability and the conditions of the housing market.

The earthquake risk scenario in Peru and South America

In order to assess the earthquake risk scenario, it is necessary to analyse events that occurred in the past and obtain evidence of highly susceptible seismic areas. Levels of vulnerability and the capacity to deal with the situation must also be identified.

Seismic activity is a recurrent feature all along the South American coastline, a highly seismotectonic area associated with the subduction or friction of two tectonic plates: the Nazca plate and the South American plate. The former extends from Panama to the south of Chile and the South Atlantic. Most of the seismic phenomena in Peru are the result of the interaction of these large plates, which in turn form part of the Pacific Ring of Fire where most of the Earth's seismic activity is concentrated. Most of the seismic activity in Peru, as well as and the volcanic activity in the south of the country, forms part of the orogenic (mountain formation) process that gave rise to the Andes mountain range and continues to this day. The characteristics of the Andes, which run along the western part of the American continent, are associated with geological faults. Superficial earthquakes are caused by large geological faults.

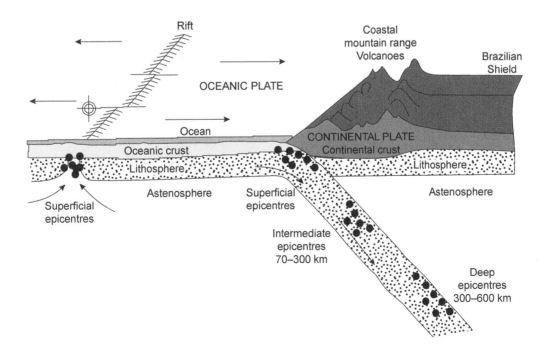

Figure 2 Seismic activity in the Andean region caused by tectonic movement

http://dx.doi.org/10.3362/9781780446721.001

The tectonic activity in the Andean region is mainly controlled by the displacement of the Nazca Plate underneath the South American Plate; the friction of both plates creates an unlimited number of tremors of different magnitudes and at different depths.

The less frequent, destructive earthquakes that occur on the continent are caused by the second seismogenic source, which tends to generate earthquakes of a lesser magnitude. However, because they are superficial, these earthquakes are just as destructive as those created by plate frictions.

History of prominent earthquakes in Peru

There is a data-base of the different earthquakes recorded in Peru, which have been compiled from different sources. Records of earthquakes there date back to the era of Spanish colonization. It is estimated that more than 2,500 significant earthquakes occurred between the Spanish conquest in the 15th century and the end of the 19th century. The strongest occurred in Arequipa in 1582, 1600 and 1868; in Cusco in 1650; in Trujillo in 1619 and 1725; and in Tacna and Arica in 1868. Although these were registered in the most important cities, the surrounding areas and neighbouring districts were also affected.

The strongest earthquakes of the 20th century were those that affected Piura and Huancabamba (1912), Caraveli (1913), Chachapoyas (1928, 1990), Lima (1940, 1966, 1970, 1974), Nazca (1942), Quiches and Ancash (1946), Chimbote and Callejon de Huaylas (1970), Satipo (1947), Cusco (1950), Tumbes (1953), Arequipa and Moquegua (1958, 1960), Silgado (1998). The second to least in strength, which registered 5–6 on the modified Mercalli scale, was recorded on 26th August 2003 in the south of Peru, Moquegua being the worst-affected area. The districts most affected by earthquakes have been Ancash, Arequipa, Moquegua, Tacna, La Libertad, Ica, San Martin, Lima, Amazonas and Piura.

Table 1 shows the intensity of seismic activity in Peru. It is worth mentioning that 55% of the tremors recorded were concentrated between 1950 and 1970, although this is largely due to more information being available around that time than previously. As the map clearly illustrates, there is considerable seismic activity along the entire Peruvian coast, the sub-Andean jungle fringe area, the central area east of Lima and the country's southeast.

Table 1 Main earthquakes recorded in Peru between the 16th and 20th centuries

Date		Epicentre	Cities affected	Magnitude
22 January	1582	Coast of Arequipa	Moquegua, Tacna	7.9
09 July	1586	Coast of Lima		8.1
24 November	1604	Coast of Moquegua and Tacna		8.2
14 February	1619	Coast of Trujillo		7.8
31 March	1650	Cusco		7.2
13 November	1655	Opposite San Lorenzo Island, Lima		7.4
12 May	1664	Ica		7.8
20 October	1687	South Coast of Lima		8.2
28 October	1746	North Coast of Lima		8.4
13 May	1784	Coast of Arequipa		8.0
07 December	1806	Opposite the port of Callao, Lima		–
10 July	1821	Coast of Arequipa	Moquegua, Tacna	7.9
13 August	1868	Coast of Tacna	Moquegua, Tacna	8.6
	1912	Piura, Huancabamba		7.0
28 July	1913	Chala		7.0
06 August	1913	Caravelí, Arequipa		7.75
02 December	1914	Parinacochas, Ayacucho	Arequipa	Strong earthquake
08 February	1916	Lima	Ayacucho, Huancavelica	Strong earthquake
11 November	1922	Caravelí		7.4
14 May	1928	Chachapoyas, San Martín		7.3
18 July	1928	Chachapoyas, San Martín		7.0
24 May	1940	Lima		8.2
24 August	1942	Nazca, Ica		8.4
30 September	1946	Pisco		7.0
10 November	1946	Quiches, Áncash		7.25
01 January	1947	Satipo, Pasco		7.5
11 May	1948	Moquegua	Arequipa, Tacna	7.1
10 December	1950	Ica		7.0
03 October	1951	Moquegua	Tacna, Arica	7.3
12 December	1953	Tumbes		7.7
	1958	Arequipa		7.3
	1959	Talara, Piura		7.25
	1959	Arequipa		7.0
24 December	1959	Highlands of Ayacucho	Río Pampas	Destructive
13 January	1960	Arequipa	Caravelí, Mollendo	7.5
	1960	Nazca, Ica		7.0
	1963	Áncash		7.0
17 October	1966	North Coast and Lima		7.5
19 June	1968	Moyobamba, San Martin		7.0
31 May	1970	Chimbote, Huaraz		7.7
	1970	Querecotillo		7.1
18 August	1972	Sachamarca, V. Fajardo, Ayacucho		5.4
03 October	1974	Lima		7.5
29 May	1990	Río Alto Mayo, San Martin		6.0
04 April	1991	Moyobamba, San Martin	Rioja	6.2
31 October	1999	Ayacucho	Chuschi	
23 June	2001	Moquegua	Tacna, Moquegua, Arequipa	Destructive

Source: Silgado, 1998. Drawn up by the author

In the last 500 years, seven destructive earthquakes stronger than 7 degrees (according to the modified Mercalli scale) have occurred in the districts of Moquegua and Tacna. During the last 80 years, five strong earthquakes have occurred in Ayacucho and another five (measuring more than 6 degrees on the Mercalli scale) were recorded in the Alto Mayo region. Despite the latent threat, the affected cities have recovered and continue attracting migrants from other areas.

It is worth pointing out that some of the strongest earthquakes that have struck Peru (measuring more than 8 degrees on the modified Mercalli scale) also caused tidal waves that caused damage all along the Peruvian coast. Silgado (1978) and Dorbath (1980) indicate that the earthquakes of 1586, 1687 and 1746 that struck the central coast, which destroyed the city of Lima, created tidal waves as high as 15–20m. The most important earthquakes in the southern region occurred in 1604, 1784 and 1868. The latter destroyed the cities of Arequipa, Moquegua, Tacna, Puno and Arica, creating 14m tidal waves (Silgado, 1978). The earthquake of 23rd June 2001 in the south of Peru caused a tsunami that destroyed numerous homes in Camana (Arequipa).

Earthquakes occurring in the mountain range covered by zone 2 (Figure 3) have collateral effects such as fractures and landslides of different types. The most frequent involve falling rocks, large blocks of fractured rock and earth that can travel over long distances and at high speeds. The combination of loose material together with the water it picks up on the way cause a debris avalanche and debris flows. The greatest debris avalanche recorded in Peruvian history was the one that buried the town of Yungay, caused by the earthquake of 1970 which killed 67,000 people in the district of Ancash.

Figure 3 Effects of seismic activity in Peru
Source: Kuroiwa, 2002: 109

The occurrence of earthquakes accompanied by landslides, running soil, debris avalanche and cracks in the ground (geodynamic phenomena associated with earthquakes) is very frequent in Peru, causing damage to people, physical infrastructure, roads, water, sewage, energy and communication networks and farming and livestock facilities, such as irrigation canals, crop plantations, barnyards and dairy plants, among others.

Zone 3 has suffered the effects of running soil owing to the confluence of soil and high water tables, destroying numerous homes, as occurred in the city of Chimbote in 1970. This kind of phenomenon is not easy to evaluate and even harder to foresee. In technical terms, ground drains represent a potential preventative measure, but would involve high costs given the technology and constant maintenance required.

Some geographical characteristics of Peruvian cities and towns

In view of its geographical location on the northwest coast of South America, Peru has the characteristics of a sub-tropical country. Influenced by the Andes mountain range, it is geographically divided into three marked areas: the coastal strip, the Andean highlands and the sub-Andean or Eastern jungle area. It has altitudes and plains as high as 6,746 m above sea level.

Since the middle of the 20th century, land occupation in Peru has been strongly determined by countryside-to-city migration processes, the construction of means of communication, and the linking up of the main productive activities. This has given rise to changes in urban growth rates and in the standard of living of the population.

People on the coast have settled in areas near ports and fishing sites, with a river as the source of water for crop irrigation purposes. City settlement, development and expansion patterns have been influenced by means of communication. Cities tended to be divided into blocks, initially with large plots that were subsequently subdivided by the owners. The main square was city dwellers' centre of gravity. The most prominent citizens would build the most solid and well-finished buildings around the square, such as the church, the municipal hall and the police station.

Coastal cities have tended to expand freely on nearly flat land with arid or limey soil. Temperatures vary between 27°C and 40°C in summer, dropping to 11°C in winter. The river has provided the construction materials for the buildings, such as cobble-stones, sand, and the reeds and trees growing on its banks. The cobble-stones have been used to pave the streets as well as in homes. Traditional constructions were built with mud and cane (adobe or 'quincha'), whereas in areas closer to the sea, they were built of timber with roofs made of wood, mud and roof tiles.

Settlements in the rural areas of coastal valleys tend to be associated with farms that have adjusted to the flat topography of the area and are situated near communication links.

In rural highland areas, the characteristic layout inherited from colonial times consists of blocks on average sized plots. More often than not they have a wide main road leading to the main square, which is usually located in the geographical centre of gravity and in the least sloping area. Administrative buildings, health establishments, the police station, the church and other public buildings are located around the square. As the towns grow, following a linear pattern along the access roads, they expand onto slopes either towards the hills or the river, increasing their vulnerability to earthquakes, landslides and floods owing to unstable soil, rugged slopes and deficient foundations. The further the houses are from the town centre, the less stable they are.

The streets tend to follow the same pattern: they are cobbled or paved around the square and then the further they are from the centre they become unpaved roads. The streets are used for rural transport; some sections consist of very narrow cart tracks and there are no long-term plans to widen them to accommodate new means of transport, resulting in a lack of routes that could be used as means of escape in the event of an earthquake.

In rural areas, houses are built in districts used for farming or livestock-raising activities; in other words, they tend to be spread out and are often very precarious. Housing is a secondary priority for farmers, who often use their homes as warehouses as well.

The materials used in both urban and rural areas are the traditional construction materials obtained from the hills and the earth: stones, rocks, straw, timber, dung, horse hair and mud for making adobe bricks and adobe or mud walls. Stones are used for the foundations and *ichu* (Andean straw) or tiles for the roof.

In northeast sub-Andean areas such as those in the district of San Martin, the urban settlement pattern is associated with the largest river ports, river confluences and existing roads. These are the main means of communication and trade upon which the development of the towns depends.

Urban patterns take the form of a quadrangular layout around a main square. As the towns grow, they adapt to the topography, which usually comprises platforms of high ground located between flood-prone land. The soil is rich in lime, clay and organic matter. There are very few public areas or open spaces to which people can escape in the event of an earthquake.

In general, the way a town is divided up is an indication of how old it is. The older the town is, the more subdivided and complex the properties. The increase in density is a result of the

division of inherited properties or partial sale of open spaces. Some plots have no access to the street except through intricate narrow passages that would make it difficult to keep track of the population in the event of an earthquake, fire or other emergency situation.

Only recently has water, sewage and energy infrastructure started to be considered an urgent need in growing urban areas. Water can no longer be taken from the river and there are not enough sites in which to dig wells; most rubbish is not biodegradable and sewage has started running down the middle of the streets towards a nearby ditch or stream, increasing the risk of infectious diseases. Towards the hills, the houses are not as close together, leaving room for small plots that may contain crops, housing and barnyards. These are built on steeper slopes protected by stone walls with no technically appropriate supports; therefore, the risk of the houses caving in or sliding is very high.

Architectural design, traditional building technology and materials

In Peru, the traditional homes of low-income households usually also serve as storehouses for their produce or for raising edible domestic animals (poultry and guinea pigs). There has been a tendency to reproduce such homes in the towns. When designing housing, consideration must be given to the need for protection from climate factors, the availability of construction materials and the cultural traditions of the people. In Andean highland areas, the houses serve as shelters from cold weather, heavy rainfall, hailstones and marked changes in temperature between day and night. In jungle fringe areas, houses are used as shelters from high temperatures and heavy rainfall and must be built in areas protected from frequently overflowing rivers. On the other hand, houses on the coast need less protection from cold temperatures as they are usually built on idle land in a humid climate characterized by high temperatures in summer, limited rainfall and, in some cases, strong winds like the 'Paracas' winds that pollute the atmosphere with dust.

The coastal strip is characterized by a lack of rain and warm temperatures, with houses that look like rectangular boxes with flat roofs. The size of the homes varies depending on the financial situation of the people living in them, but houses in urban areas are very conventional, comprising a living room, dining room, kitchen, bedrooms, bathroom and a back yard. They are usually built in stages over a long period of time, with various building materials such as wood, adobe, bricks and *quincha*. The formal structure is the same in rural areas, although the houses are more precarious and the rooms larger.

Houses in small Andean highland farming towns usually consist of a single room, built on one or two storeys. The ground floor is usually used as a storehouse, a social area and a kitchen which is shared with small animals like guinea pigs. The second floor is used as a bedroom. In rural areas, two or three buildings are built around a courtyard which has no roof (20m^2 or 30m^2). If there is a vegetable garden, it is usually located at the back of the plot or at the side of the building. Plots are usually separated by a stone fence with spiky vegetation (varieties of cactus or *huaranguillo* planted for security purposes). One of the buildings usually has two doors: one leading to the street and the other to the inside courtyard. The other buildings only have one door to the courtyard. Access from the street is through a large gate in the front wall.

The limited ventilation in the homes, misused toilets – if any – and the habit of using the bedroom as a kitchen and a guinea-pig farm at the same time, mean that poor sanitation is a way of life.

In sub-Andean jungle fringe areas in the east, housing design is closely linked to the climate, characterized by heavy rainfall, high temperatures and floods caused by overflowing rivers. Consequently, the houses are built on stilts or in high areas, with a wide open design or with large windows for ventilation and comfort. The roofs are very high, made of timber covered with palm leaves to make them waterproof.

The empirical development of appropriate technologies in each region is the result of the search for, and adaptation and combination of materials that are easily available in the respective areas. The precarious nature of the homes is due to the replication of inappropriate construction systems and lack of adequate maintenance. In addition, migrants tend to follow construction practices customarily used in their native areas and these may be inappropriate for their new settlements.

The use of traditional building materials, systems and techniques bears a relationship with local natural resources that are economical for housing construction. Stones are used for the foundations; and mud or adobe, cane, bricks, timber and cane with mud (like 'quincha'), among other materials, for the walls, used in different combinations and with different techniques to tie them together. Logs, 'ichu' straw, roof tiles and, more recently, corrugated plastic sheeting are used for the roofs.

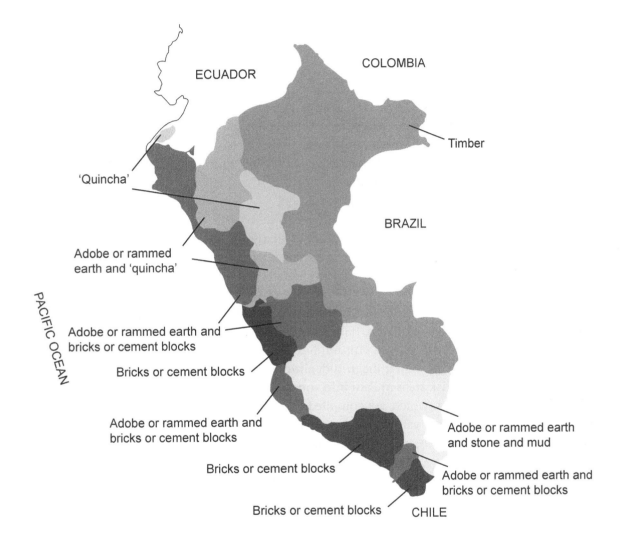

Figure 4 Traditional building materials in Peru

Source: Monzón, 1990

Construction systems that employ earth and cane are most common in the most poverty-stricken urban and rural areas of the country. Bricks and concrete blocks are employed in the main cities. Timber is used in abundance for construction in both urban and rural areas of the Amazon region.

In more economically developed cities like Lima and Tacna, buildings are made of bricks or concrete blocks. In Arequipa, 'ashlar' stone is the predominant resource, whereas adobe and bricks are used in other districts on the coast. In inland districts such as Puno, Cusco, Apurimac, Huancavelica and Ayacucho, most buildings are made of adobe or stone and mud. In two districts, Tumbes and San Martin, cane and 'quincha' are the main construction materials. Timber is clearly the most common resource in the Amazon region.

Table 2 (see p.25) compares the suitability of the materials used in reconstruction processes in different regions. However, consideration must be given to market-related factors. An example of this is the higher value placed on improved 'quincha' after the earthquakes in San Martin, contrasting with the current tendency to build brick and cement housing in this region, as imposed by the market in recent years.

Land occupation as a vulnerability factor

In some cases, houses are destroyed by earthquakes or other destructive phenomena, whereas in other cases only minor damage occurs, if any. Although destruction is inevitable in extreme cases, in the majority of disasters there is a great difference in the level of destruction witnessed both between settlements and within settlements themselves.

This indicates that beyond the characteristics of the phenomenon itself, there are two key factors that determine the extent of the destruction: the quality of the land on which the houses are built, and the quality of the construction.

The characteristics of potentially destructive phenomena and the quality of the soil and construction are undoubtedly key factors in analysing disaster risks from a physicist's perspective. However, if we also analyse the social processes that led to land occupation and the reasons why people continue using such construction methods, as well as the institutional or collective risk management capacity, then we can develop a more comprehensive approach: risk management.The development problems caused by adverse direct and indirect impacts of disasters on people's living conditions, habitat and economy, reveal the need to find out more about the causes of such occurrences. This implies previous knowledge of the origin of disasters and the factors that influence their magnitude, intensity and impact.

In order to divide the risk areas in Peru into zones, we drew up maps based on the occurrence of destructive phenomena, which are compiled in the INDECI Atlas. However, there are also maps based on information gathered about disasters (occurrence of phenomena, number of victims, degree of destruction, etc.), such as the DESINVENTAR data-base (see www.redesdegestionderiesgo.com).

Significant progress has been made in Peru in terms of studies and methodologies related to risk evaluation and risk-zoning, but these mostly refer to a 'physicist's' evaluation of risks in cities and, to a lesser extent, in the countryside.

With respect to the cities, micro seismic zoning studies have been conducted by the National Engineering University (UNI) and other universities, and geological studies have been conducted by State institutions (IGP, INGEMET). The Sustainable Cities programme, implemented by INDECI with the assistance of the UNDP, has conducted micro zoning studies on the main disaster risks in each of the main cities in Peru. The studies need to be updated in order to improve them and incorporate new urban settlements or settlements that were not initially considered. These studies include the urban micro zoning maps that are featured later in this book.

Table 2 Viability of construction materials in relation to climate, resources, traditions and vulnerability

Material	Zone	Natural resources and environment	Traditional construction	Suitability in relation to vulnerability to disasters
Quincha	Coastal strip	Not enough material available. The cane used is imported from Ecuador. However, the climate is appropriate for planting different varieties of bamboo (cane).	Rudimentary cane constructions date back to pre-Hispanic times. The Spaniards introduced woven cane, using it in homes and churches. There are traditional constructions in Lima, La Libertad, Tumbes, Piura, Trujillo and Arequipa. Cane is currently used in rural areas.	Very appropriate owing to its great flexibility during earthquakes. Another advantage is that it provides comfort in hot and humid areas. Architectural designs from the viceroy period (sixteenth to eighteenth centuries) need to be recovered and new designs developed.
	Andean highlands	Not enough material available at altitudes of 1,500 m above sea level and above.	Few communities use it. There are some traditional buildings in Cajamarca. In cities with modern means of communication, people prefer to build with bricks and concrete.	Not much cane is available in Andean highland areas. Despite its good structural performance, its thermal qualities are not appropriate for low temperatures.
	Northeast	There are some varieties of bamboo (cane) and the climate is favourable for introducing new varieties or improving existing plantations.	Mud and adobe are traditionally used in urban areas. 'Quincha' is used in rural areas of Loreto, San Martin and Yurimaguas. At the present time, 'quincha', timber, adobe, mud and bricks are used. Bricks and concrete are predominant in urban areas.	It has a very satisfactory performance in earthquakes and is also appropriate for hot and humid climates. The roofs can be made of woven palms.
Adobe	Coastal strip	Used on a large scale. It depletes the quality of farmland.	This building tradition dying out in urban areas. Used in very poor housing or in rural areas.	With cane or electro-welded mesh reinforcements it can have a good seismic performance and has good thermal properties.
	Andean highlands	There is enough appropriate mud for use in areas where other construction materials are unavailable.	Building with mud is a tradition because it is an abundant material. It is used at altitudes of 1,500 m above sea level and above, where access by road is very limited.	With cane or electro-welded mesh reinforcements it can have a good seismic performance and has good thermal properties which are much appreciated in this area.
Concrete blocks	Coastal strip	There are sufficient materials and they can be distributed easily thanks to the extensive road network.	The use of concrete blocks is increasing because they are inexpensive, easily manufac-tured and are being used for reconstruction purposes. Widely used in Marcona, Tacna and Moquegua. Concrete is easy to introduce in rural and urban areas.	They perform well in earthquakes. Their thermal properties are limited. A bio-climatic architectural housing design is required, e.g. higher ceilings.
	Andean Highlands	They perform well in earthquakes. Their thermal properties are limited. A bio-climatic architectural housing design is required, e.g. higher ceilings.	Their use is expanding. They have already been introduced in La Oroya, Cerro de Paso, Junin, Huanuco, Cajamarca and Cusco.	They perform well in earthquakes. Their thermal properties are fairly limited.
	Northeast	No materials available.	This construction material is being introduced, but its use is not appropriate owing to the limited materials in the local area, which raises construction costs.	They perform well in earthquakes. Their thermal properties are limited. An architectural design with higher ceilings is required.

In addition, during the last two decades, some specialized NGOs (mainly Practical Action and PREDES, the Disaster Prevention and Study Centre) have promoted risk evaluation studies in urban and rural communities, including the following:

- background to disasters
- evaluation and zoning of hazardous areas (river beds and gorges, unstable slopes, slippery areas, etc.)
- evaluation of the quality of the land prior to construction (stability, compactness, etc.)
- location of structures with respect to risk
- evaluation and zoning of constructions according to the types of material used and degree of deterioration
- risk awareness among communities
- proposed mitigation measures
- analysis of risk reduction and disaster response agents and their roles.

Risk studies and evaluations are essential instruments for development planning and for reducing risk in general. The main difficulty encountered so far is that these are rarely used, either because they have not been circulated widely enough, or are not properly appreciated, or because people simply do not know who should use them and how. Hence the need for a dissemination and implementation strategy which should take into account the following:

- the participation of local leaders and officials in identifying and analysing risk
- experiments through pilot programmes and projects
- dissemination to local authorities and officials and their successors
- dissemination to organizations and the population in general (via the media)
- approval of the proposals and their incorporation into local plans and budgets
- design and implementation of risk reduction standards and policies.

Vulnerability, poverty, market and housing policies

Peru has a population of about 28 million people, concentrated mainly on the coast and, to a lesser extent, in the highlands and jungle. An important sector of the population live in areas highly susceptible to earthquakes, situated in the districts of Tumbes, Piura, Lambayeque, La Libertad, Ancash, Lima, Ica, Moquegua, Arequipa, Tacna, Ayacucho, Cusco, Puno, San Martin and Amazonas.

In 2001, the housing deficit in Peru was estimated at 1.3 million units, of which 77% represented inadequate housing and 23% no housing at all. Consequently, there was a demand for 110,000 new housing units a year, 80% of which were built through self-construction (Romero, 2002).

The vast majority of the population has been unable to gain access to private housing. Of the people in need of dwellings, 42% live in extreme poverty and 26% belong to the lower-middle class, meaning that 68% of the population cannot afford private housing.

In general terms, the housing market is divided into three segments which, according to the main agents involved and the kind of capital used, can be classified as follows: i) formal private sector; ii) subsidized government sector; and iii) informal and non-institutional sector (Lopez, 1996; Abramo, 2003).

The formal private sector follows the logic of the market; therefore, the market seems to be the social mechanism that links prospective owners of land and housing with the demand. In Peru, this sector operates in the main cities (Lima, Arequipa, Trujillo, Cusco) through various real estate agents. Houses are also built on demand; that is, people contract small construction companies to build their homes. Between 1996 and 1998, 12–14,000 homes a year were built by the formal construction sector.

The subsidized government sector. Although the State undertook mass housing construction projects during the fifties, sixties and eighties, this activity was then neglected. At the present time, the State has a few subsidized programmes with a small impact, such as 'Techo Propio', whereby the buyer makes a $400 contribution to receive a $3,600 bond.

The informal and non-institutional sector. People gain access to land informally, invading State or private properties that are usually not being used. These people tend to build their own homes, with the help of their families and reciprocal social practices, resorting to construction foremen or civil construction workers for stages that require skilled manpower. Self-construction, which covers nearly 68% of the homes built each year in Peru, takes place without any technical advice from competent professionals or any supervision by the authorities.

Poor people settle on steep slopes, sand, river banks, alluvial plains, areas with geological faults, slippery slopes or insufficiently compacted land. Their homes are usually precarious, owing to the quality of materials and deficient construction techniques they use, and the subsequent deterioration of the building due to lack of maintenance. This situation is directly related to the lack of alternative mechanisms available to poor families in the urbanizing market to gain access to housing. As a rule, these families spontaneously occupy land in the cities or their outskirts that has neither been urbanized nor categorized for use, using their own area-distribution criteria (streets, public areas, housing, etc.). In addition, they build their homes empirically and progressively (over a period of about 15 years), obtaining their basic services by negotiating with politicians or through public demonstrations. As a final step, only the minority that have title deeds (less than 20%) 'regularize' their situation by obtaining building permits and technical files and completing other formalities that should have been fulfilled previously. This 'regularization' does not allow for any control over the quality of the housing. The quality of housing in rural areas and villages is even worse, as peasants tend to place little value on their homes.

Poverty and self-construction are key factors in explaining the vulnerability of the population, and disasters tend to increase poverty. For example, the most recent studies on poverty in Peru revealed that the main reason given by non-poor families in rural areas for becoming poor was what they mistakenly called natural disasters. As mentioned in the introduction, disasters are not natural; they only occur when vulnerable conditions already exist. According to the National Housing Survey of 2001, 17% of the families living in the countryside had been badly affected by disasters (Chacaltana, 2004).

Despite the situation described above, the public sector should be considered highly responsible for this state of affairs, particularly in terms of inadequate risk management, for the following reasons.

- It lacks a housing policy that takes into consideration a planned and rational use of land for the poorest sector, hence the spontaneous land occupation motivated by need. Furthermore, there is no rural housing policy.

- There is no policy that incorporates prevention and better quality housing criteria. There have been no credit facilities available to poor people, until recently through the Materials Bank.
- Property regularization or land tenancy processes are extraordinarily slow and they tend to endorse occupations in hazardous areas as they fail to take into account micro seismic zoning in the cities. The lack of title deeds in Peru becomes even more complicated as many houses are transferred or sold informally. When a disaster occurs, it is difficult to determine whether the victims are the original owners, tenants or temporary occupants of the homes, as was demonstrated after the August 2007 earthquake in Ica.

References

Abramo, P. (2003) *A cidade de informalidade. O desafio das cidades latinoamericanas*, Río de Janeiro: Zette Letras – LILP.

Chacaltana, J. (2004) *Can poverty be prevented in Peru?*, Lima: CIES.

Kuroiwa, J. (2002) *Reducción de desastres Lima 2002*: UNDP.

Monzón, F.M. (1990) *Vivienda Popular*, Practical Action Publishing – CIDAP.

Romero, M. (2002) 'La visión del Colegio de Arquitectos frente a la problemática de la vivienda', in CIPUR Perspectivas y posibilidades para una política de vivienda en el Perú Lima.

López, E. (1996) 'Los aspectos conceptuales que se desarrollan se basan' in La vivienda social: una historia. Guadalajara: U de G.

Silgado, E. (1998) *History of the strongest earthquakes in Peru (1513–1974)*', Lima: Ingeomin (now the Geological, Mining and Metallurgical Institute INGEMMET).

CHAPTER 2

Research and application of earthquake-proof technology

This chapter contains an analysis of the most recent research into earthquake-proof technologies, following the 1970 earthquake in Peru. The housing reconstruction processes undertaken by NGOs in Peru over the last 15 years are also analysed. The experience of Practical Action and its partners in the reconstruction process will be analysed in the next chapter.

Reconstruction experiences in this country have not been suitably analysed. The 1970 disaster was the most significant given its magnitude, when entire cities and rural towns that had been devastated by the earthquake and the mudflows had to be rebuilt. Subsequently, disasters associated with the El Niño phenomenon (mudflows and floods) gave rise to other reconstruction experiences, as did the earthquakes that prompted the intervention of NGOs during the nineties. A common characteristic of nearly all these experiences is that they were not properly systematized.

The 1970 earthquake, which caused the death of 67,000 people in the district of Ancash, involved a material reconstruction process based fundamentally on foreign aid and planning from the top. The long-lasting aid provided to the victims caused serious distortions, because the local market was substituted by the massive amount of foreign aid and people developed a collective dependence on assistance. Initially, measures were implemented to make houses safer as a result of effective planning of land use, installation of drainage facilities in the cities – reducing the threat of liquefaction – and the use of construction techniques implemented in accordance with the standards and regulations accepted by specialized institutions. Consequently, the reconstruction led to radical changes in the main cities, as adobe was replaced by concrete in housing construction, large plots of land were expropriated and redistributed to poor families, wider streets were designed, and the areas most likely to be affected by earthquakes, mudflows or overflows were set aside as free areas. In rural areas, on the other hand, the conditions prior to the disaster were reproduced, building with adobe and using the same techniques as before.

The 1970 tragedy brought about substantial changes in the country, resulting in the formation of the National Civil Defence System. Decades later, it was proved that the redevelopment of the region was limited by a lack of local initiative, the absence of citizen participation mechanisms and the fact that the original risk factors were recreated, particularly by reoccupying the land that had been buried by the mudflows for housing purposes.

During the eighties, reconstruction after disasters became a prerogative of the State and, through it, of private companies, focusing mainly on productive and urban infrastructure. Not much attention was given to housing, except in the case of State housing loan programmes and the implementation of housing projects as a result of the destruction caused by the El Niño phenomenon. For example in 1983, Sencico Chiclayo relocated the town of Chochope under an agreement with the Development Corporation of Lambayeque, rebuilding 100 dwellings using adobe reinforced with cane (earthquake-proof), following the recommendation of the National Institute for Housing Research and Standards (Ininvi). Likewise, under the 1985 agreement between Sencico Chiclayo and Dejeza, the relocation, mitigation and construction of 300 dwellings took place in the new Ciudad de Dios, located at the crossing of the Cajamarca and Pan-American highways, as they had been affected by the construction of the Gallito Ciego dam.

During the nineties, NGOs, other bilateral cooperation institutions and State entities gradually ventured into housing reconstruction experiences. Practical Action, Caritas and the Disaster Prevention and Study Centre (Predes) in San Martin were the pioneers in this respect. Also, within the framework of the United Nations International Decade for Natural Disaster Reduction, some universities carried out seismic risk studies in Peru's main cities.

Research on earthquake-proof technologies for reconstruction processes

In Peru, research on architectural designs and structures using alternative technologies is being carried out by prestigious institutions like the National Engineering University (UNI) and the Pontificate Catholic University of Peru (PUCP), which are playing a community service role by collaborating on specific projects related to seismic events and the training of future professionals.

In its *Tecnia* magazine, the UNI publishes research work by well-known national experts in the field of anti-seismic civil engineering. The PUCP also publishes its research work, as well as the results of laboratory tests on soil and the resilience of materials.

The universities in affected areas (Private University of Tacna, San Agustin of Arequipa, Huamanga of Ayacucho) also have laboratories and special equipment for testing soil and other risk management and mitigation applications. The intervention of professionals resident in seismically active areas will encourage commitment to their region and they will be able to guide the disaster management process in the immediate future, through their professional work or university teaching.

The following are some of the experiences of inter-institutional research work on construction technologies:

- The '10 x 10' Project in Moquegua, whereby the UNI and the National Standardization, Research and Training Service for the Construction Industry (Sencico) built 10 conventional houses (living room, kitchen-dining room, bathroom and bedroom), using various techniques and materials. The Seismic Research and Disaster Mitigation Centre (Cismid) conducted the soil surveys. Under an agreement, the Moquegua Benevolent entity participated in the selection of beneficiaries and provided a site for the concrete block factory, whereas the wooden frames for the 'quincha' were made in private workshops. Through this experience, alternative technologies were promoted among the local community, some of them fairly sophisticated.
- Ininvi, which has been taken over by Sencico, intervened in the reconstruction of housing destroyed after the 1990 earthquake in Rioja and Moyobamba. The technology employed was prefabricated 'quincha'.
- Based on the studies conducted by the former Ininvi, Sencico carried out construction with adobe, meeting the requirements established in the Technical Building Standard NTE E. 080 Adobe. Together with the Materials Bank, Sencico published the primer 'Improved adobe houses' in 2001, which was distributed free of charge and refers to such aspects as the location of buildings, the foundations and the manufacture of adobe and mortar for the walls as well as their reinforcement and protection against dampness.
- The Agency for International Development (AID), the Development Corporation of Lambayeque and the Catholic University of Lima (which participated in the testing of materials with the laboratory staff), were involved in the housing reconstruction process in Piura after the El Niño phenomenon in 1983. The conventional houses consisted of

a living room, a kitchen-dining room, a bathroom and two bedrooms, with concrete foundations, reinforced adobe walls and galvanized iron roofing.

- The Regional Seismic Research Centre for South America (Ceresis), together with other institutions, implemented a pilot project for Ica, Ancash, Cusco, Moquegua, Tacna and La Libertad, to apply reinforcement techniques to existing constructions in order to delay their collapse after earthquakes. They resorted to prototypes to reinforce adobe houses with electro-welded mesh in the corners, simulating columns and beams. It was discovered that this technique could not be applied to poor quality soil or to houses with more than two storeys, no foundations and low density walls. The technique was quickly learnt and applied by local construction workers. This technique is also recommended for new constructions and has been applied by other institutions for reconstruction purposes, reducing costs by enhancing the structural design.

- UNDP, Sencico and the Italian Government, under an agreement with the University of San Agustin in Arequipa, built 97 houses in Arequipa in order to conduct soil and structural design surveys. Each house had two bedrooms and was built of reinforced adobe and electro-welded mesh. Sencico was in charge of training local construction workers and officials.

- Foncodes built schools as part of the reconstruction project in the south. In order to make the project sustainable, it provided training to the population on the construction of water and sewage infrastructure and irrigation facilities, using local manpower.

As a result of the construction experiences and research into alternative materials, the following standards have been incorporated into the National Construction Regulations:

1. Technical Building Standard NTE E102, Standard design and construction with wood, Ininvi.
2. Technical Standard 339005, concrete elements, bricks and blocks used in bricklaying, Indecopi, Lima, 1984.
3. Technical Standard NTE E070, bricklaying, Ininvi, Lima 1982.
4. Standard E 080, for improved adobe constructions.
5. Prefabricated 'quincha', an unconventional construction system R.M. N° 106-95 MTC/15 VC 21-03-1995.
6. Technical town-planning standard NTE U. 190, town-planning adaptation for disabled people. Ministerial resolution 069-2001 MTC (Ministry of Transport, Communications, Housing and Construction).
7. Technical Architectural Standard NTE A. 060, architectural adaptation for disabled people, 2001.

Reconstruction experiences, use of non-traditional technologies and participation of NGOs

The intervention of NGOs in housing reconstruction processes began as a result of the two earthquakes that occurred early in the nineties in the department of San Martin. In view of the magnitude of the disasters and the impossibility of meeting the needs of the victims, Caritas and Predes decided to implement housing construction processes using 'quincha', bearing in mind its intensive use in the area and the research under way to enhance the quality of constructions and materials.

The basic strategy consisted of training the target population to disseminate the alternative technology implemented, so that it would be accessible to as many people as possible, creating a multiplier effect. The idea was to encourage the community to participate in the work, provide training on construction techniques and use local resources for housing construction purposes.

After the earthquake of 12th November 1996, which affected the borders and coastal areas of the departments of Ica and Arequipa, a reconstruction experience was undertaken in which links were established between institutions like Caritas, the Red Cross and Predes. Using similar strategies to those implemented in San Martin, houses were built with improved 'quincha' and cement blocks in the farming areas of Nazca and the mining areas of Caraveli.

The most successful reconstruction experiences were in the rural settlement of Pajonal, where all existing houses had been destroyed. Risk studies were carried out, revealing that the cause of the total destruction was the location of the settlement in an old alluvial bed. Consequently, the settlement was relocated a few kilometres away and the houses were built of improved 'quincha'.

After the earthquakes that occurred in the south of Peru in 2001, different institutions were involved in the reconstruction. Below are the actions and non-traditional construction technologies employed by those institutions between 2001 and 2005.

- The Resettlement Support Programme (PAR) of the Ministry for the Promotion of Women and Human Development, together with the Swiss Agency for Development and Cooperation (SDC), intervened in Ayacucho after the earthquake of June 2001, working in coordination with the community to allocate land and hold workshops on construction training and psychological recovery. Houses were constructed, using technical procedures to improve the resilience of adobe constructions, mainly relating to the foundations, the size of the adobe bricks and the binding of joints or unions. The homes have two bedrooms, a multi-purpose storeroom and a bathroom with water supply. They have cement foundations, adobe walls and a wooden roof covered with concrete tiles. As a special feature, double-height walls were offered (6m), leaving spaces for an intermediate roof structure, so that the beneficiary could eventually expand the home. The second-storey wall would be built or financed by the beneficiary. The construction work was directed by a resident engineer in charge of three simultaneous projects of 25 houses each.

- SDC established a network of micro enterprises incorporated by the beneficiaries, with the quality control supervised by the firm Tejacreto S.A., which supplies local roof tiles for projects run by this and other consortia.

- For its part, GTZ-Germany worked in the Andean highlands of Arequipa, rebuilding houses with reinforced adobe and electro-welded mesh in the corners of the buildings, in order to prevent them from collapsing immediately in the event of an earthquake. The population was trained by specialized technicians from Sencico. The average floor area of the two-room houses was 36m^2.

- In 2001, Chile's Hogar de Cristo donated 100 prefabricated wooden houses to Moquegua, of approximately 30m^2 with galvanized iron roofing. However, the material used and the design proposed were not the most appropriate for the local climate, owing to their limited thermal insulation properties. People prefer to use these houses as storerooms.

- Caritas participated in Moquegua's reconstruction after the 2001 earthquake. Through its emergency programme, it built 23m^2 houses with prefabricated 'quincha' in Lima and assembled them on the site, with 'fibraforte' roofing, at a cost of US$1,200 per unit. Through food incentives, the target population was encouraged to build the foundations, assemble the panels, install the roof and lay the polished cement floor.

- The Promotion of Life Institute (Vidaprom), with the assistance of Intermon-Oxfam Spain, implemented a project to reconstruct community buildings and 26 adobe houses. They introduce improvements in the structural designs, such as adequate foundations (stone and mud 0.80m deep and 0.60m wide), bricklaying (0.37m × 0.37m × 12.5m walls), and reinforcement buttresses (recesses) in all the corners and across the walls. Below are some of the standards applied to improve the quality of adobe structures:
  - The maximum length of a wall between two buttresses is no more than 10 times its thickness; that is, walls between two buttresses are by no means longer than 4m.
  - The maximum height of a wall is no more than eight times its thickness.
  - The sum of the widths of the doors and windows is delimited by the two buttresses and must not be more than 30% of the total length of the wall.
  - The end spans will be centred and must be no larger than three times the thickness of the wall.
  - Lintels must be equivalent to one and a half adobe bricks, in other words the support at each end must be 0.60m.
  - The tie beam partially confines the wall and supports the beams in order to eliminate the effects of the upper wall cracking and crumbling.
- The Disaster Prevention and Study Centre (Predes) worked in Islay and Castilla (Arequipa) and Sanchez Cerro (Moquegua) after the June 2001 earthquake. The intervention was aimed at rural communities, building a basic multi-purpose single room housing module of 24m² with water and electricity connections. Improved 'quincha' was used in Islay and Castilla because the resources were locally available and the modules could be built quickly. The module has concrete foundations, a sawn timber structure, 'quincha' walls lined with cement mortar, metal doors and windows and a cement floor and pavement. In Sanchez Cerro, 30m² two-bedroom houses were built, with concrete foundations and improved adobe walls reinforced with electro-welded mesh in the corners both inside and outside. The roof is timber covered with galvanized zinc roofing. An alliance was established with Sencico for the purpose of training the beneficiaries. Urban growth towards safer areas was encouraged.
- The Materials Bank. After the earthquake of 23rd June 2001 which affected the south of Peru, particularly the districts of Arequipa, Moquegua and Tacna, the Government allocated 100 million Nuevos Soles for housing reconstruction purposes. This sum was channelled through the Materials Bank, an entity experienced in the implementation of mass housing programmes.

The programme to build 10,000 houses was implemented with a long-term soft loan payable over 20 years. One of the basic requirements to obtain the loan was the presentation of an 'Earthquake Victim Certificate' issued by the relevant municipality and a certificate issued by INDECI confirming the land was safe to build on. These conditions had priority over traditional

requirements like proof of income or guarantees.

The houses were designed by a professional architect or engineer, depending on the needs of the family concerned. The Materials Bank decided to use industrialized construction materials, which offered economic advantages when purchasing significant volumes as well as an adequate transport and distribution system. The houses had an average area of 35m², including a bathroom. They were built of machine-made bricks, with reinforced concrete foundations, columns and roofs. The self-construction method was used, with the help of skilled manpower and the technical assistance of an expert.

The population showed a clear preference for the brick and concrete construction, even though other construction techniques were on offer. The reconstruction programme was completed within approximately one year and was later expanded by the central government in office at the time.

The following are some key considerations when ensuring the safety of houses:

Adobe	Quincha	Tapial (compact mud)
The location, type of soil, bearing capacity and vibration of the soil. Only build on good quality land, considering the limitations of the seismic resilience of adobe.	The type of soil, method for carrying out basic tests in the field to define the type of foundations and to evaluate the quality of the aggregates on the site (salt, sulphates) and of the water used for the mix.	The method for defining the foundation.
The method for defining the foundations.		The earth to be used.
The type of binding for the adobe bricks and the distance between joints.	The type of reed, depending on what is locally available.	The width of the walls and the maximum permissible height.
The proportions and size of the adobe bricks.	The type and proportions of mud mortar and plaster.	Corner bracing.
Reinforcement with electro-welded mesh on the corners, on both sides, with ¼ iron bolts every 60cm.	Mesh reinforcements for guaranteed bracing.	Distance between the joints in each section.
Incorporation continuous ring beams all around.	The most resilient type of wood.	Guaranteeing the traction stress, which is equivalent to its own weight by compression.
The appropriate coating to prevent the erosion of the foundations and walls by water.	The quality characteristics required when selecting the materials.	The necessary protection in terms of the roof and lining, to reduce the vulnerability to water.
The direction and speed of the wind and the level of rainfall must be taken into consideration for the shape of the roof.		
The height required for the walls to prevent them from collapsing.		
Whether the water is hard or soft.		

Some conclusions

Since 1970, various public and private research centres have intensified their work aimed at improving the quality and resilience of housing in general, particularly those buildings made of 'quincha', adobe and cement blocks, which are mainly used in poor areas for self-construction. As a result of this research work and its validation through the construction of a limited number of houses, there are technologies available in this country for building housing appropriate to the conditions of each region. However, these technologies were not applied on a mass scale until the early nineties, when NGOs and the State intervened in reconstruction efforts following the earthquakes that occurred in the districts of San Martin (Alto Mayo), Ica (Nazca), Ayacucho, Arequipa, Moquegua and Tacna.

It is worth pointing out that the main achievements of this research work are directly related to the safety of the homes, particularly in terms of their resilience to earthquakes. Bearing in mind the close relationship between the intensity of an earthquake and the resilience of the construction materials, the importance of the latter is evident. Obviously an earthquake that destroys concrete constructions is more intense than one that only destroys adobe buildings.

Although there are still thousands of badly built adobe and 'quincha' houses that have not been modified despite the research work, at least the technical instruments for doing so are now available. Some of the most relevant findings relate to the quality and dimensions of the materials to be used and the structural reinforcements associated with establishing adequate foundations and the reinforcement of joints and/or bindings.

The reconstruction processes undertaken by NGOs and public organizations have been more efficient, calling upon the community to undertake the reconstruction work, implementing participatory mechanisms, making arrangements for the allocation of land and the selection of beneficiaries, coordinating with other institutions, providing training in construction and using local resources to build the houses.

Although in some cases access to soil surveys has been gained through inter-institutional coordination, such studies usually need to be organized before the construction programmes begin. Findings from these not only make it possible to identify various hazards, but also their possible impact, depending on the characteristics of the soil and whether the constructions are located in urban or rural. Consequently, they provide guidelines for institutions and individuals on building in more suitable areas or on ways of reducing risks in unsuitable areas. Risk assessments can have different levels of complexity, to be defined by means of a preliminary survey based on information available in the area and how the buildings have performed during previous earthquakes.

Historically houses tended to be designed by the technicians in charge of implementing the project, without consulting the population or their leaders. In urban areas, conventional houses were used for the purpose they were designed for. In rural areas, however, people adapted the rooms to suit their needs, using them as storerooms for their harvest, for drying grains and for other farming activities.

The reconstructed houses most valued by the target population in rural areas are those that respond to local requirements, consisting of two rooms which are used as bedrooms or a storeroom and a bathroom with water supply. Local materials are generally used, together with improved traditional building technologies. Nevertheless, some projects have used inappropriate materials for the local climate; in these cases, people have moved out of the homes and are using them as storerooms or, in extreme cases, have abandoned them altogether.

In general, workshops have been set up to manufacture adobe bricks, blocks, tiles and other building components, supervised by foreign experts. Although training the victims is a good mechanism for ensuring the maintenance and replication of the houses, it would have been better to train some members of the target population to become leading constructors, through more selective complementary activities.

It must be borne in mind that training in construction techniques is usually insufficient. Training and advice on organization and community management skills would be just as effective in reducing risk, if not more so, in order to guarantee the replication of the programmes in future. Furthermore, technical training does not necessarily take into account the fact that some materials and equipment may not be available once the programmes are completed; this is another important aspect to be considered for their sustainability.

It is important to obtain a better idea of how the community can participate, particularly the women. Some of the experiences described have given rise to significant changes in the leadership of communities and households, which is not usually analysed in the evaluation of such experiences.

Finally, although the cooperation relationship between public and private institutions has improved significantly, it is evident that local governments are still not sufficiently committed to the reconstruction processes. The participation of local governments is a mechanism that could have a greater impact if the criteria for designing policies, standards and initiatives were aimed at reducing risk to a minimum, improving people's participation or reducing the costs of reconstruction processes. The reconstruction experience in Nazca after the earthquake of 12th November 1996 was an exception, as in this case the provincial municipality actively contributed to the reconstruction in rural areas.

CHAPTER 3

Practical Action's post-disaster reconstruction work in the Amazon, highland and coastal regions of Peru

Between 1990 and 2003, Practical Action intervened in the areas affected by the earthquakes that occurred in the districts of San Martin (Alto Mayo), Ayacucho (Chuschi, Uchuyri and Quispillacta), Moquegua (capital city) and Tacna (La Yarada). The purpose was to help the poverty-stricken families affected by the disaster to rebuild their homes and reduce their exposure to risk.

With the participation of the victims, Practical Action built a total of 708 houses in Alto Mayo, 213 houses in Ayacucho and 259 houses in Moquegua and Tacna, making a total of 1,180 houses. The people themselves built 2,000 more houses in San Martin and in Ayacucho, Moquegua and Tacna some houses have been extended using the same technology.

Figure 5 Areas where Practical Action's reconstruction projects were carried out

The reconstruction in the jungle (Alto Mayo), in the Andean highlands (Ayacucho) and on the Pacific Coast (Moquegua and Tacna) took place bearing in mind the expert contribution of professional training and technological research centres in Peru, which through their

http://dx.doi.org/10.3362/9781780446721.003

research, have helped improve construction techniques and materials such as 'quincha', adobe and concrete blocks during the last few decades. The contribution of Practical Action to the reconstruction processes consisted of the use of participatory methodologies for risk management purposes and the application of appropriate technologies.

For mass dissemination purposes, flexible architectural designs were made to suit the limited family budgets, efficient housing construction processes were organized with community participation, and the community's management skills were developed to improve their standard of living.

Beneficiary families were selected among those that were living outdoors or in provisional shelters after their homes had been destroyed by the earthquakes; also, efforts were made to teach them building skills that would be valued on the construction market as well as ensuring the safety of their homes. More family integration was encouraged and the women, who were the protagonists of the reconstruction experiences were encouraged to build up their self-esteem.

The initial experience in Alto Mayo, which gained international acknowledgement, focused on the use of improved *quincha* technologies, the manufacture of construction materials (light roof tiles) and the participatory management of the reconstruction process by the community and local institutions. The experience involved recovering and using some of the materials from the destroyed houses, which reduced costs and meant that a larger number of houses could be built. The experience also validated a more earthquake-resilient technology to counteract the devaluation of technologies based on the use of adobe, and it emphasized the effectiveness of a high level of local participation.

The experience in Ayacucho involved the application of technologies to improve the seismic resilience of adobe, referred to as improved adobe, within the context of a return to this area by people who had previously been driven away by terrorism and military repression and the possibility of an earthquake occurring. The experience was initially aimed at providing risk management training and organizing the population; subsequently, it focused on building housing and water supply systems.

The reconstruction experience in Moquegua and Tacna focused mainly on the construction activity itself, owing to time conditions established by the donors supporting the project. Improved adobe was used, as well as cement blocks in areas where more resilient housing was required. The roofs of the houses were consistent with the traditional architecture. Workshops were organized to prepare the materials and, to promote and facilitate the participation of women, day-care centres were established to look after their children.

The most prominent aspects of the latter experience were the variety of materials used (mainly adobe and cement blocks) and the diversity of designs. Not only were the designs adapted to the uses, customs and budgets of the target population, but the size of the areas varied as well, depending on whether the settlements were located on slopes or in areas with more land available.

Institutional roles and risk reduction

From a risk management point of view, reconstruction not only involves material reconstruction but also the creation of institutional conditions and organizations to reduce vulnerability, therefore the joint efforts of local institutions are required.

In principle, the State should play the role of coordinator in reconstruction processes, through provincial and/or district municipalities that have been assigned key responsibilities and should therefore provide information, strategies and physical, professional and legal resources, particularly for relocation purposes, physical-legal integrity and building permits. When this has not occurred, the institutions involved in the reconstruction have made informal arrangements with each other to obtain the required information, complement resources and avoid duplicating efforts. This has prompted them to resort to universities and institutes that have specialized information or studies on micro seismic zoning (indicating how different types of soil behave in earthquakes).

Although the new housing designs and structures substantially improved their safety, it was also necessary to identify the characteristics of the land in the affected and surrounding areas, in order to take complementary preventive steps. This could involve modifying the foundations or carrying out protection work and, in extreme cases, relocation. An important indicator was the damage suffered by the different types of houses nearby and the interpretation of the causes of such damage, so that adequate decisions and measures could be taken. In some cases it was only necessary to review the existing studies and technical inspections carried out by geologists and other experts in order to evaluate the danger, with the participation of representatives of the different communities. In other cases where the destruction was obviously greater, soil assessment studies were required.

In Alto Mayo, the institutional presence of Practical Action prior to the occurrence of the disaster allowed for a better relationship with the community, as well as a better selection of beneficiaries and the establishment of alliances with local institutions and other NGOs that complemented and provided continuity to the intervention. The identification and selection of the most vulnerable people was made easier with the help of institutions like the Catholic Church, which carries out pastoral work in extremely poor areas. Local community organizations also helped to establish lines of communication, information and coordination with the local people and institutions, such as the role played by the Public Welfare organization during the survey of the most affected and most economically vulnerable people after the 1990 earthquake in Rioja, Alto Mayo.

In Ayacucho, the local government (municipality) helped to transport materials and to install public toilets. The intervention began with a long process of familiarization, followed by training on construction techniques and organization geared towards risk management. The quality of the soil and the proposed designs were then assessed, taking into account the evident prominence of adobe, given its accessibility and suitability to the climate. The formation of management committees to control the supply of safe water in some areas of Chuschi and Quispillacta ensured a good supply for the direct beneficiaries and the efficient maintenance of the rebuilt facilities, but this did not fit with the municipality's desire to manage the sanitation system as a whole. The municipality wants to manage and distribute the water in order to benefit other areas and to reduce losses. However, the people did not trust the municipality as it had been incapable even of providing public toilets.

In the most recent experiences in Moquegua and Tacna there were considerable differences between the experiences themselves and in comparison to previous cases. On this occasion, Practical Action intervened in an area where it was evident that the adobe houses would easily crumble – this being the predominant material used in very old housing.

The intervention in Moquegua originally took place in areas where State housing loan programmes had been implemented, where the lack of damage to the homes built in that sector proved the safety of the soil. It was then decided to work on slopes to give support to some extremely poor families, where the need to replace adobe with cement blocks was evident. In addition, work was carried out in an area established by the municipality for the relocation of victims, based on the recommendations of a survey conducted by specialized institutions. Here the land was of varying quality, therefore in some cases the foundations were reinforced and concrete blocks were used as the most technically appropriate solution.

In Tacna (La Yarada), the intervention took place in relatively safe areas. This being a farming area, the fact that the houses were spread out made it unfeasible to carry out individual soil assessments, therefore safety criteria were applied during the construction of foundation pits and foundations were reinforced with iron bars. Annex 2 contains a description of the systems employed in each place.

A relevant aspect in all these cases was the informal nature of the properties, as the majority of the victims had no title deeds; however, local institutions and organizations provided them with accreditation without creating any conflicts. The extreme poverty of the beneficiaries and the limited value of their plots meant that a tenancy arrangement was virtually impossible. With the help of the central government, the municipalities subsequently legalized these situations.

Housing designs

The cost, area and type of materials to be used were determined when the reconstruction projects were drawn up and the housing designs were based on those parameters, including the modules or parts of the houses to be built.

During the initial stage of the projects, it was necessary to obtain some alternative housing designs so that the participating population could make adjustments or modifications and select the one they preferred. Future housing was designed bearing in mind the differences between the countryside and the city, local traditions, the availability of local materials and people's preferences.

To achieve this, preliminary research work was conducted to determine the basic characteristics of a local dwelling and the typical equipment required. Subsequently, housing design workshops were held, with the participation of the beneficiaries, so that they would understand that the basic module to be built had the potential to be gradually extended. A further description can be found in Annex 4.

Local customs and familiar architecture, materials and technologies were considered in the design, in order to respond to the expected use and extension of the homes.

The final housing models designed for the population of Chuschi, Uchuyri and Quispillacta in Ayacucho were based on the research carried out in the architectural design workshops conducted by the Practical Action team for the Alto Mayo project and the Ayacucho project. In these workshops, it was determined that the most appropriate housing would offer one or two bedrooms, a 'marka' or storeroom for the harvest (which could also be used as a bedroom), a kitchen outside these rooms, near a patio, and an outside bathroom.

Table 3 contains details of the houses designed in the Alto Mayo workshops and the research on the typology of traditional housing in Ayacucho. These models were applied during the reconstruction process in Ayacucho and, in view of their flexibility, they were also used in Moquegua and Tacna, with slight changes in the shape of the roof.

For the basic modular design, a 3m x 3m square area was considered. This is a flexible size compatible with any use, in which it is easy to fit a group of rooms to comprise a small housing module, and is flexible enough to be adapted to any topographic relief; because of its square shape, it has the required structural security and stability, in addition to being simple enough for the population to understand and replicate.

Based on this design, several housing modules were built which we shall refer to as R1, R2, R3 and L. R1 has certain variations in the longitudinal measurements, ranging from 1 to 1.5m, depending on the topography of the land. Table 4 contains a summary of the types of houses designed based on the basic module, corresponding to the number of family members and their capacity to build the house within the terms established during the projects.

Table 3 Housing models used by Practical Action for reconstruction purposes

In Alto Mayo, the work took place with the population in order to develop housing that best suited their lifestyles. This consisted of two bedrooms, a living-dining room and a bathroom.	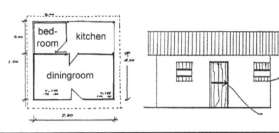
In Ayacucho, the characteristics of existing houses were considered in the design of one- or two-room modules. The rooms consisted of a bedroom, a kitchen and a barnyard. The kitchen could either be separate or adjacent to the living room-bedroom. The L-shaped and Straight model 2 was chosen for the reconstruction.	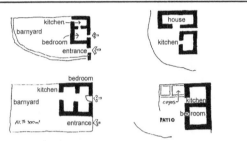
The model had to be adapted to the rugged topography, resulting in smaller spaces being used for small bedrooms and the kitchen. This served as an inspiration for the Straight model 2 subsequently applied in Chuschi (Ayacucho).	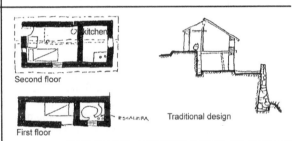
Another adaptation to the rugged topography was the Marka type housing: The bottom floor consists of a patio and a storeroom for the harvest. The second floor is at road level and contains the front door that leads to the actual dwelling and above that, there is an area for drying grain and straw.	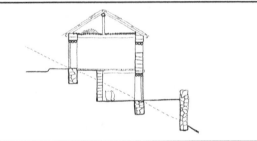
A more sophisticated and larger model was designed for the construction of community sites. In highland areas, community centres are used for cultural and social activities.	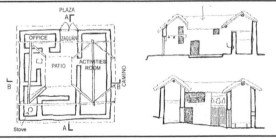
For Andean highland areas, foundations that prevent the soil from settling are recommended, and footings that prevent the damp from damaging the base of the walls. A ring beam is used so that there are no beams resting directly on the wall.	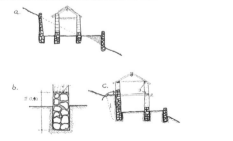

Table 4 Area distribution in houses under reconstruction

Type	Description	Diagram
Module R1	Two sizes: 3m x 3m and 3m x 5m. The use of this module is similar to that of R2. Beneficiaries tend to divide the room into two with a curtain: one to be used as the living room, kitchen and storeroom and the other as a bedroom.	
Module R2	This was the module that best suited the needs of the population and was neither modified nor expanded.	
Module R3	Although this module does not match the typical housing in the areas of intervention, the people adapted to it. The modules built with cement blocks had different bindings, given the structural potential of this system.	
Module R4	This module had to be divided by a wall into two rooms: one for the original family and the other for when one of the children started a family of their own. The module was used for different purposes, including dwellings, storerooms and workshops. When the module was extended, this usually involved adding another room by using two of the walls that form the L-shape, in most cases building additional walls and a provisional roof.	

This basic plan was used for the reconstruction projects in Ayacucho, Moquegua and Tacna, adjusting it to the type of technology applied and the shape of the roof. These basic modules allow the beneficiary to develop a living space more in-keeping with their cultural environment and customary use. In cases where module R3 was applied (three rooms), the tendency was to secure one of the rooms for another family or use it as a storeroom.

In the structural design, consideration was given to the recommendations made aimed at dealing with the deficiencies found in traditional adobe houses, such as inadequate foundations for earthwork, soil settlement differences, dampness at the base, humidity in the house, erosion caused by rain, beams leaning directly on the wall, deficient plastering and the lack of wall anchors. (See the next box, Recommendations.)

Recommendations for overcoming the deficiencies in traditional adobe housing

- Differential settlement. A structural flaw in the foundations due to an earth tremor or due to existing deficiencies in the foundations (structural design or errors in the construction process), as a result of which the walls lose stability and crack. To overcome this deficiency, it is necessary to know the bearing capacity of the soil in kg/cm^2 and the loads to be transmitted, applying design load rules in force in Peru, depending on the materials to be used for the foundations, footings, walls, roof and so on. It is also essential to know how the soil behaves in earthquakes, that is, whether it is compressible and sensitive to liquefaction.

- Humidity at the base of the walls. This occurs when the wall is in contact with the soil due to a lack of footing or when it has not been adequately protected from the dampness of the soil or the rain. As a result, the walls weaken, lose their verticality or crack. To overcome this, water drainage should be anticipated and the foundations and footings should be made waterproof with adequate materials, the walls should be protected by pavements, floors and skirting in the lower part and adequate plastering.

- The selection of unsuitable earth when making the adobe bricks. This problem does not emerge immediately. However, in some cases a low resilience of the walls to erosion by the rain or the wind was observed, as a result of a badly prepared mix or poor construction technique. The earth selected for making adobe should not be mixed with organic material (roots); it should consist of sifted clay and sand, so that no cracks appear during the first tests. In addition, it should contain barley or rice straw or 'ichu', to provide an adequate degree of cohesion.

- Walls that are not quite horizontal and vertical, owing mainly to the use of defective adobe bricks or a lack of quality, care and precision in the construction and the absence of corner reinforcements and beam supports (ring beam). To overcome this correct procedures should be followed for making the adobe. The mud, prepared by one or two people after stamping on it and adding straw, must be moulded and un-moulded in the shade, if possible, and on a flat surface to prevent the bricks from warping. The way they are dried and piled for storage and transport purposes is also important. Adobe bricks half the size should also be made for the corners, joints or buttresses. The roof beams placed on the walls must be fitted to the lintels of the doors and/or windows with No. 8 wire and four rows of adobe bricks.

- Too many openings or the bad positioning of doors and windows in the walls weakens their consistency, causing more cracks during earthquakes or a fault in the soil support. During an earthquake, the structure behaves asymmetrically with respect to the seismic wave. In Peru standard E-080 for adobe indicates that there should be no more than one door or window opening in each wall and their width should always be less than their height.

- Inadequate thermal and acoustic insulation. Galvanized zinc sheeting or similar materials do not provide thermal insulation for the changing weather conditions in Andean highland areas. The use of 'ichu' is recommended as a good insulation material that grows in abundance in areas above 4,000 m above sea level. It is estimated that 'ichu' remains in good condition for about five years. Galvanized zinc roofing should be replaced by 'ichu' and compacted mud to obtain a roof with good thermal insulation.

Training workshops on construction designs, materials and techniques

The projects implemented by Practical Action involved three kinds of workshops related to construction technologies: design, preparation of materials and construction techniques. Learning by doing was the purpose of these workshops; therefore, apart from learning the theory, the people also built their homes.

Training on housing designs involved meetings with groups of target families who were taught basic notions of architectural design and construction, based on a critical review of the design of their previous housing.

The dynamics of the design workshops were geared towards the participating group identifying their own lifestyles and suggesting their housing requirements by drawing an architectural diagram. Family members were encouraged to participate in this process.

The participants were taught how to draw simple plans of their future home. They also used coloured blocks to identify each area in the home. After holding several design workshops, typical 30m^2 models were developed, based on which the beneficiaries could select the one that best suited their needs.

The models described above were used in the projects implemented in Moquegua and Tacna.

The materials workshops were also relevant, although because of their nature they involved smaller groups of people who were selected according to different criteria, prioritizing young people and women. In Alto Mayo and Ayacucho, the workshops were aimed at making roof tiles.

In Moquegua and Tacna, the material production workshops (roof tiles, cement blocks and other components) encouraged the women and young people to jointly organize production; they facilitated the participation of mothers who were restricted by their family responsibilities (creating child day-care centres and dividing the work according to capabilities).

The main objective of the training workshops on construction techniques was to teach the people working skills so that by the end of the workshop, the beneficiaries would be capable of building their own houses, extending them in the future, and acquiring construction skills that would eventually serve as another source of income.

Working methods were developed whereby the participants could improve on their traditional techniques. Local construction foremen were trained to supervise the work and disseminate the improved technology, and efforts were made to use locally available construction materials.

The training workshops also served as a practical demonstration open to the entire population. In Alto Mayo, the training took place by means of the construction of a community site. In Ayacucho, a model house was built. In Moquegua and Tacna, there were small demonstrations focusing on production and use of construction components: adobe, cement blocks, copings, roof tiles, etc.

In Alto Mayo, the workshops began with an invitation to a leader of a group, a presenter or the president of the reconstruction committee, backed by household visits to encourage the participation of family members. According to José Luis Mego Pandero, a social outreach worker on the Alto Mayo project, the acceptance and participation of those involved in the workshops was fundamental in ensuring the progress and achievement of the project's goals. In Ayacucho (Chuschi, Quispillacta and Uchuyri), it was necessary to have a Quechua-speaking communicator participate in the sessions throughout the construction process; local authorities did not participate.

The construction foremen trained in Alto Mayo became the instructors and implementation managers of the projects in Ayacucho, Moquegua and Tacna.

Annex 3 contains a graphic description of the components and systems employed (improved 'quincha', adobe and cement blocks).

Risk management workshops

These workshops were designed at the beginning of the reconstruction processes, in order to:

- improve the self-esteem of the victims, recognizing their citizens' rights, skills and relevance in the reconstruction and local development process
- involve the community as a whole, rather than only the direct beneficiaries of the houses, in the planned project activities in order to encourage the replication of the technologies employed and improve risk management skills
- reduce risk in the reconstruction process by establishing links between various public and private institutions and local and regional community organizations and trade unions.

The following were among the main contents of the workshops:

- An analysis of the causes of the disasters, particularly the vulnerable conditions that comprise the most relevant factor in all cases.
- An analysis of the capacity and strategies for strengthening local organizations and institutions, based on the definition of the roles and responsibilities of government and non-governmental organizations and institutions and the identification of their strengths and weaknesses.
- The participatory design of risk reduction plans and proposals, considering prevention works, the policies of the different institutions and the mechanisms aimed at ensuring the participation of various community organizations.

The development of the workshops was uneven, owing to the different financial possibilities and priorities in the various project sites. In San Martin and Ayacucho, the workshops were processes that began prior to the construction activities and carried on during the construction phase, whereas in Moquegua and Tacna the organization time for the risk management workshops was very short, so they were events rather than processes.

Organization and sustainability of the construction process

When selecting the beneficiary families, priority was given to those that had suffered the greatest material losses and were the most vulnerable socially owing to their poverty and the structure of their families (more elderly people, children and households headed by women). The selection criteria were as follows:

1. Collapsed housing
2. A victim certificate issued by local authorities
3. The possession of plots of land with available areas of at least 30m^2 located in a safe (not high-risk) site
4. Legally obtained title deeds
5. Local residents
6. No other house owned in the main city (for Ayacucho and Tacna)
7. Not borrowers or beneficiaries of any other credit or aid institutions

The assistance of authorities, local churches, municipalities and aid institutions was obtained in making the selection; information was cross-referenced to make sure that help would go to the people most in need. In addition, the Practical Action technical team conducted surveys which were processed and analysed to determine the type of housing module to be built. The information requested in these surveys aimed to establish:

1. the structure and characteristics of the family concerned (ages, health conditions, relationships), to enable an accurate assessment of the housing characteristics required
2. the location and characteristics of the available land
3. urban development conditions (pavements, roads, water and sanitation networks, etc.)
4. the number of family members who could participate in the construction.

In establishing the relationships between technicians and participants and between the participants themselves, it was necessary to get the families to commit to the following:

1. active participation of the families at every stage of construction
2. the contribution of construction materials in good condition or transported from nearby quarries
3. that the newly built property would not be sold within a period of at least five years.

To implement the housing construction project in Alto Mayo, groups of local people were formed which proved to be useful for organization and mutual assistance purposes, encouraging discussions and decision-making and following up the agreements reached. These groups were in charge of sanctioning those who failed to turn up or to collaborate. As each group consolidated itself, its members transferred the knowledge they had acquired to those who had just started working, thus successfully achieving the project's objectives.

In Ayacucho, Moquegua and Tacna, the working groups were organized based on their reciprocal community aid tradition referred to as *aini. Aini* is an Inca tradition of reciprocal work, whereby members of a family group help with each other's crops or construction of each other's homes. They use the term *minka* when mutual work is carried out for the benefit of the community, such as a warehouse, a road or a bridge (Great History of Peru, 1999).

The construction of each house took between three and four months. Initially, only immediate family members participated in the construction, but later some families requested the assistance of other relatives (who did not necessarily live in the area) and neighbours to carry the aggregates, transport the adobe bricks or cement blocks and pile them, and sift the aggregates. In view of the effort required for this kind of activity, skilled manpower had to be hired locally for some families comprising only women or elderly people, who were unable to work continuously.

In all four projects, the performance and participation of the families diminished once the roof had been built on their houses. In some cases, according to their standards, they considered the houses to be finished. Besides, many of them had to return to their jobs or productive activities. Consequently, not all the houses had plastered walls or finished floors.

In some cases, the project's budget included the construction of bathrooms with septic tanks and water networks; in others, these were built with the materials contributed by the community itself, as occurred in Chuschi, Quispillacta and Uchuyri (Ayacucho).

There were cases in which the beneficiaries were tenants who did not own their own homes, as occurred in Chenchen in Moquegua. After the disaster, when they had nowhere to live, they decided to take up residence on some available land. They were included in the project when the municipality granted them the required authorization.

In all the projects, Practical Action promoted and set in motion participatory models that were clearly approved by the target population.

In Alto Mayo, Practical Action based its work on the theory that its intervention should form part of a sustainable productive development strategy for the region in the medium and long term. In Ayacucho, Moquegua and Tacna, the community's organization and technical skills were developed at training workshops on construction and risk management and through their participation in construction activities.

During the interventions, it was important to bear in mind the psychosocial impact on the population, due to the trauma of losing family members coupled with the loss of the possessions they had acquired during a lifetime of hard work and hardships. Efforts were therefore made to strengthen values such as solidarity and group awareness, making the people intervene in the reconstruction process. Obviously it took longer to build houses in this way than if conventional methods had been used. However, the additional time helped to improve the sustainability of the intervention and contributed to the recovery of people's self-esteem.

Channels of communication with the population were used, promoted by the technical teams participating in each project. The local radio, verbal messages and workshop meetings, among other methods, proved to be effective communication mechanisms.

The participation of the community had a strong influence on:

1. the acquisition of new organizational skills by community members and their ability to prepare materials and learn construction techniques
2. the strength of community organizations and their capacity to negotiate with institutions and authorities
3. the help provided to members of the population who because of their age, gender, family burden or state of health could not carry out work that required great strength and physical effort.

Participation in the construction was influenced by the following factors:

1. the structure and composition of the family, as well as leadership within the family
2. the level of instruction and preparation family members had received in activities similar to construction
3. the family's livelihoods when the disaster struck; this would affect to what extent they could participate without neglecting their productive activities.
4. the type of community organization and community leaders in the area, as well as their improvement based on risk management workshops.

The tables in Annex 4 contain a synthesis and graphic summary of the work carried out in the design workshops, the training on construction, the organization by teams, the levels of expertise within the workshops by gender and by age, the monitoring of participants and the contributions made to the improvement of the housing design.

Sustainability

The difference between the interventions of Practical Action and construction companies not only involves the housing characteristics, but the sustainability of the projects once they are completed. In the construction process promoted by Practical Action, users appropriate the construction technology for this type of housing and place more value on it because they know the houses are safe, long-lasting, more economical and easy to replicate or expand and/

or guarantee housing facilities for other families who require them. This appropriation not only cheapens the housing construction costs, but the techniques learnt can subsequently be applied to the maintenance or expansion of the dwelling.

The sustainability of the 'quincha' houses built in Alto Mayo was recently verified. 'Quincha' houses continue to be built in rural areas, whereas in urban areas 'quincha' is gradually being replaced by conventional materials like bricks and cement. In Ayacucho, the houses are still being acknowledged as an improvement on the traditional design; although poverty has prevented them from being replicated on a large scale, in general the community has improved its initial facilities. The projects in Moquegua and Tacna are too recent to have felt this impact, however the beneficiaries have improved their homes (see Annexes 2 and 4).

Nevertheless, there is a significant difference between the experiences in Ayacucho and Alto Mayo, which was perceived years later. Although in both cases the population participated in the construction of their homes, the local contribution made by both the people and the authorities in Alto Mayo seems to have resulted in a greater appropriation of the houses and the technology. Whereas the people in San Martin maintain and add to their homes, in Ayacucho people have a passive attitude towards their homes, so they tend to deteriorate owing to the occurrence of unexpected meteorological events. Rather than restore them at a virtually insignificant cost, the expectation of foreign aid seems to prevail.

This difference in attitude cannot be attributed to cultural differences, as there are also examples that indicate the contrary: whereas in Alto Mayo there are passive attitudes to the destruction caused by the floods in water and sanitation systems, in Ayacucho the water supply systems technology has been appropriated. These differences could therefore be attributed to the management of the reconstruction processes.

Collateral activities and proposals

In Alto Mayo, the reconstruction plan, which included the reconstruction of housing and services as well as improving local organization and the livelihoods of the affected families, was drawn up with the participation of several institutions. In order to implement and promote the plan, radio programmes were broadcast on local radio stations, photograph exhibitions were held, articles were published in nationwide newspapers and television spots were also used. In addition, courses were offered to constructors and demonstration sites were built.

Complementary projects to promote environmental protection were also implemented, including the installation of an agro-forestry nursery to replace the timber used for construction purposes. Proposals and messages were broadcast on local radio programmes, local outreach workers were trained and a display panel on reforestation was prepared.

Furthermore, a number of specific reconstruction projects were designed for the area, such as the housing projects for the worst-affected districts (Soritor) and training projects for local constructors on improving the non-industrial production of lime and roof tiles.

In Ayacucho, under an agreement with the municipality of Quispillacta, equipment was donated and training was provided to local youths who acquired the know-how and skills to continue and/or replicate the production of roof tiles.

References

El Comercio. (1999) *Great History of Peru*, Lima, CARSA Group.

CHAPTER 4

Lessons and recommendations for disaster risk management and reconstruction

A reconstruction proposal that is not capable of partially or totally removing the risk disaster would be unsatisfactory. Reconstruction must involve institutional and community participation that inspires synergies based on solidarity, self-esteem and local identity, in order to heighten people's awareness of their rights and obligations. This will ensure that they can adopt the technologies and guarantee the construction of good quality housing in safe areas and conditions in the future.

Practical Action has promoted a housing reconstruction process geared towards self-construction, incorporating technologies that help improve the quality of housing and generating local skills and institutional conditions to provide sustainability to the process. The key factors to consider to achieve this are the location of future housing, construction technologies and capacity building.

Institutional strategies and alliances for the reconstruction process

A reconstruction project can be more effective if links are established between local institutions that are capable of playing a vital role in the process.

In general, municipalities are not prepared to provide organization facilities or information on the victims, fulfil legal relocation requirements, clear physical-legal impediments, or lead the relocation and reconstruction processes. It is necessary for mayors and authorities to be informed of construction technologies that respond to local needs and resources, as occurred in San Martin, or to receive technical studies from institutions like *Cismid* and Indeci, as occurred in Moquegua.

As regards the affected population, the reconstruction should be approached in a holistic manner, not only from the point of view of the dwelling place. In addition, new opportunities must be created to develop risk prevention skills and to make inhabited areas safer, strengthening the commitment of the inhabitants to the process. Improving and diversifying livelihoods is a fundamental and viable part of the reconstruction process, as new opportunities arise for production and local services. Recycling rubble, the production of materials and construction activities can become mechanisms that trigger the development of new skills among the victims so that they can earn more income and recover their losses. A wider promotion of the project in nearby areas is advisable to encourage the replication of the construction techniques.

Alliances between the institutions or organizations that carry out reconstruction work or projects in areas affected by earthquakes, complementary resources and activities can be arranged, intervention sites and types can be more fairly spread across the area concerned, better areas can be selected for relocating the beneficiaries, housing designs can be improved, physical-legal encumbrances can be cleared, and so on.

Alliances not only make the intervention easier, but local agents are more committed to their development and continuity.[1]

For risk management purposes, it is necessary for the municipal institutions involved in territorial management to consider existing risks to their plans and programmes. Risk assessments and risk-zoning, making construction licenses conditional on suitable soil types, prohibiting construction and urban renovation in risk areas, and providing appropriate relocation sites for the victims with appropriate physical and environmental sanitation infrastructure, are some of the means and used instruments to achieve this.

To improve the quality of self-construction processes, specialized technical advice is required; therefore, it is recommended that the institutions involved establish alliances with prestigious universities or specialized institutes to conduct micro seismic-zoning studies, soil surveys and laboratory tests.[2] Local universities that have architecture, civil engineering, sanitary engineering or electrical engineering programmes can also participate in the design workshops and support the reconstruction work.

To gain access to immediate and reliable information for the selection of the beneficiaries most in need, alliances must be established with NGOs, municipalities and grassroots associations permanently involved in the affected areas.

For construction training purposes, strategic alliances are required with specialized institutions (e.g. Sencico) or some universities that have staff trained in the teaching of construction techniques. These institutions could certify trainees who reach minimum standards of instruction, so that they can enhance their qualifications and develop a potential line of work for the future.

Surveys: risks and capacities

An adequate survey of the area earmarked for intervention is required as the best starting point for subsequent actions. The survey must include an assessment of physical damage, present or future risk, an analysis of the livelihoods of the affected families, the institutional and organizational capacities available and the availability of materials. The feasibility of rebuilding in the affected area or the need for relocation should also be evaluated, if relevant.

The assessment of institutional and organizational capacities is essential because on the one hand, it provides guidelines for the institutional alliances mentioned previously and on the other, it allows for the establishment of adequate relationships with the victims and the different organizations involved. The analysis of capacities can include different types of capital (human, social, political, environmental, productive, etc.).

The experience revealed a considerable difference between reconstruction activities in rural and urban areas. Large areas of land and sufficient natural resources are available in the countryside but not in the cities. However, activities in rural areas are restricted by limited access, communications and markets and the timing of reconstruction work depends on the productive seasons and processes, whereas in urban areas more definite and immediate timelines can be established.

When planning construction activities in exposed areas, seasonal variations in the area and extreme weather conditions must be borne in mind, as well as the availability of facilities to carry out the construction work. Delayed reconstruction could cause health problems or additional material losses.

In the surveys it is important to take into consideration that indiscriminate tapping of natural resources, and the occupation of apparently 'free' areas for housing and farming purposes could have an impact on environmental degradation, contamination, desert encroachment and the watershed balance, among other things. Such activities have transformed many populated areas into places that are highly vulnerable to destructive phenomena. Therefore, an adequate survey must not be limited to the reconstruction site itself, but should also examine the potential impact of surrounding areas on the site's vulnerability, in relation to the different threats. Reconstruction programmes implying the use of timber should consider incorporating reforestation programmes that could serve for housing construction in the future, for stabilizing slopes or as live barriers against high river levels or mudflows.

In established towns or cities where new buildings will increase the population density, planning is fundamental for decision-making. When evaluating the risks (it is very useful to know the causes of disasters), consideration should be given to the different threats, the complexity of destructive phenomena (mudflows, landslides, soil liquefaction, tidal waves) and land occupation processes, particularly those factors that pose the greatest risk and those influenced by surrounding areas. Consequently, it is important to consider the morphology of the sites proposed for new settlements and to analyse the stability of the slopes and the quality of the soil. In such cases, training will need to be provided on different housing designs and on reinforcing traditional dry-stone walls to stabilize slopes and terraces to prevent them from being eroded by rain.

During the last few decades, substantial progress has been made with respect to the assessment of risk or danger. This is described below, as it could prove useful to the engineers and technicians involved in reconstruction processes.

The micro map of hazardous zones[3] is the result of the survey of natural phenomena threatening an area and its expansion zones, drawn up after analyzing the history of disasters

Table 5 Sectors according to the danger level

Degree of danger	Characteristics	Examples	Use restrictions and recommendations
HIGHLY DANGEROUS	Natural forces and their effects are so great that man-made constructions cannot resist them. If a phenomenon occurs it could cause 100% losses The cost of reducing such damages is so high that the cost-benefit ratio makes urban construction impossible.	Sectors threatened by avalanches and sudden mudflows Sectors threatened by proclastic or lava flows Watercourse beds that originate from the summit of active volcanoes and areas affected by mudflows. Sectors threatened by landslides. Areas threatened by flooding with a great hydrodynamic force, speed and erosive power. Sectors alongside V or U-shaped bays threatened by tidal waves. Soil with a high probability of generalized liquefaction or soil likely to collapse in large proportions.	The use of such areas for urban purposes is forbidden. It is advisable to use them as ecological reserves, outdoor recreation or for growing plants with a short cycle.
DANGEROUS	Although natural hazards are great, effective measures can be taken to reduce damages at acceptable costs, using adequate techniques and materials.	Although the threat is reduced considerably in strips alongside highly dangerous sectors, the danger is still great. • Sectors where high seismic accelerations are expected due to the geological characteristics • Slowly inundated sectors that remain under water for several days. • Occurrence of partial liquefaction and expansive soil.	The use of such areas for urban purposes is permitted once studies have been undertaken by experts experienced in identifying the level of danger and establishing the boundaries with the previous sector. Recommended for low urban density purposes.
AVERAGE DANGER	Moderate natural hazard	Intermediate quality soil with moderate seismic accelerations – Sporadic slow flooding	Appropriate for urban purposes. Normal geological research.
LOW DANGER	Areas with a low expansion or seismic waves Where there is little likelihood that an intensive natural phenomenon or a gradual fault in the ground will occur.	Flat or slightly sloping land, rocks or dry compact soil with a high bearing capacity High land not prone to flooding, far removed from slippery land or hills, not threatened by volcanic activity or tidal waves.	Ideal for high density urban purposes and for essential buildings like hospitals, schools, police headquarters, fire stations, etc.

that have already occurred (earthquakes, landslides, floods) and specifying the level of danger, as shown in Table 5: 'Characteristics of zones according to danger level'.

The topography and slopes in selected areas will influence the construction costs and the most advisable decisions regarding the choice of site. Table 6 offers guidance regarding the recommended use for different degrees of slope.

Expert geologists can interpret aerial photographs and study the geological structure of an area to determine the occurrence of external geodynamic phenomena like landslides, erosion and avalanches. Should no specialized professionals be available, an empirical appreciation and immediate intervention is required so that decisions can be taken over whether to rebuild in the same place or relocate the destroyed settlement, by examining the soil and subsoil exposed by the event and following the recommendations in Tables 7 and 8. Also, the level of the water table (subsoil water) must be checked to make sure it is not superficial.

Table 6 Slopes, urban development characteristics and recommended use

Slopes	Characteristics	Recommended use
0–5%	Reasonably flat, adaptable drainage, stagnant water, regular sunshine, limited visibility, controllable erosion.	Low urban development cost, management of superficial drainage. Risk of liquefaction associated to a high water table and limey or sandy soil.
5–10%	Small to medium slopes, adequate ventilation, constant sunshine, average erosion, easy drainage.	Medium density construction, streets laid out diagonally at level curves to ease drainage.
10–15%	Soil accessible for construction, earthwork, irregular foundations, wide visibility, variable drainage.	Parallel streets at level curves, higher cost, earthwork and installation of infrastructure. Terraces.
15+%	Incalculable cost of urban development, extreme slopes, fragile foothills, bleached out and strongly eroded areas, good views.	Too many difficulties to plot roads and prepare land for building. Conservation, reforestation, recreation.

Source: Bazant, (1983): 128

Table 7 Types of subsoil, their characteristics and recommended use

Subsoil	Characteristics	Recommended use
Sedimentary and clastic	Plant sediments accumulated in swampy areas, lime, gypsum, solgema, iron mineral, magnesia, silica sand, sandstone, travertine, conglomerate.	Farming, conservation and recreation areas, very low density urban development.
Igneous and eruptive	Crystallization of a rocky body, melted. Extensive, fine grain stony texture, colite, obsidian, andesite, basalt. Intrusites, relatively thick and uniform, granite, monzonite, diorite and gabro.	Construction material, medium to high density urban development.
Metamorphic	Re-crystallization of igneous rocks or sedimentary rocks. Formed by high pressures, high temperatures and mineralizing vapours. Marble, quartzite, slate, shale.	Raw materials for industrial use, low to medium density urban development.

Source: Bazant, (1983): 130

Table 8 Types of soil, their characteristics and recommended use

Soil	Characteristics	Recommended use
Limestone	Very powdery. Fine grain when damp and clumps when dry.	Light construction. Serves as construction material.
Rocky or sandy	High compression, impermeable, hard, difficult for foundations and drainage.	Medium density construction, streets plotted diagonally at level curves to ease drainage.
Sandy	Low compression, regular for septic systems. No construction of erosion is anticipated.	Light construction and in areas with low density urban development. Danger of liquefaction in case of earthquake.
Clay	Very fine grain, smooth and powdery when dry and rather plastic when damp. Prone to erosion.	Not recommended for constructions. Infrastructure breaks up. Good material for highways or adobe bricks.
Sandy, clay	Thick grain of a sticky consistency, prone to erosion, medium resilience.	Easy drainage, medium density constructions.
Limey	Erosion problems, acceptable resilience.	Inappropriate for septic systems. Medium density construction. Danger of liquefaction.
Gravelly	Low compression, good permeability.	Low height and low density construction.
Muddy, marshy	High compression, impermeable, poor drainage, abundant flora and fauna.	Natural ecological conservation area. Construction should be avoided.

In areas with heavy rainfall, drainage canals must be envisaged and it is advisable to keep torrents and alluvial cones free for mudflows. In jungle fringe areas, it is not advisable to build in low areas prone to flooding or landslides. Where only flood-prone areas are available, the possibility of building on raised platforms using stilts should be studied.

Table 9 shows techniques used to protect slopes prone to landslides or erosion caused by mudflows (Medina, 1991).

Type of materials

The choice of materials must respond to the local tradition, the resources available in the area and the given material's behaviour in both structural and thermal comfort terms. Efforts must be made not to deplete existing natural resources, teaching the beneficiaries to replace the materials extracted. In areas where the amount of cane and timber available is insufficient, the population can be encouraged to develop forestation programmes.

Using recycled materials from collapsed buildings for reconstruction purposes is valid because this allows a larger number of houses to be rebuilt and at a lower cost. However, people need to know that the quality and durability of the houses may be limited. In that case, the materials must be selected very carefully. In addition, joints between recycled timber columns must be made impermeable to prevent them from rotting and so must the foundations.

With respect to the use of materials, improved 'quincha' proved to be adequate for the coastal and sub-Andean areas owing to its thermal qualities, cost and the supply of materials. It is not recommended for cold areas.

In the southern part of the country, the construction of adobe modules in rural or semi-urban areas proved to be the most suitable in terms of the costs, materials and available space.

Table 9 Recommended methods of erosion control

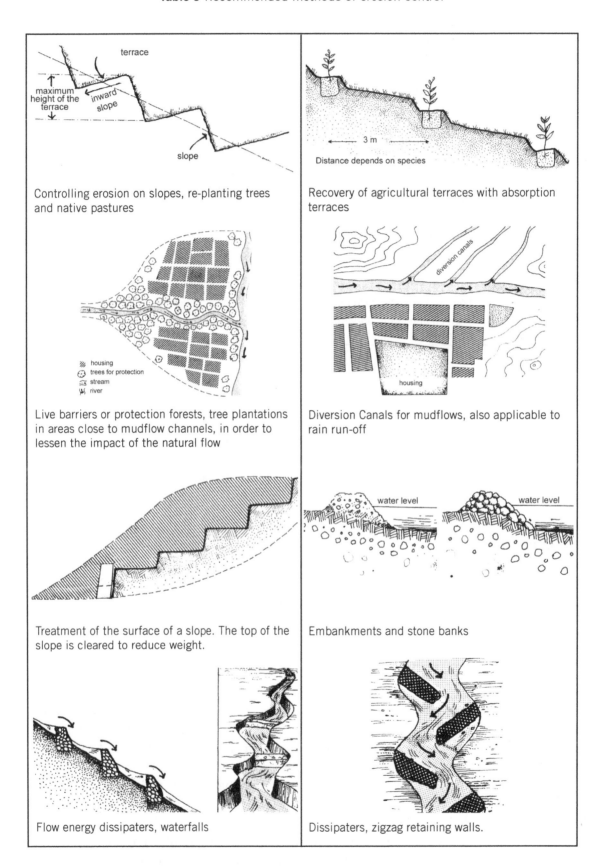

Controlling erosion on slopes, re-planting trees and native pastures

Recovery of agricultural terraces with absorption terraces

Live barriers or protection forests, tree plantations in areas close to mudflow channels, in order to lessen the impact of the natural flow

Diversion Canals for mudflows, also applicable to rain run-off

Treatment of the surface of a slope. The top of the slope is cleared to reduce weight.

Embankments and stone banks

Flow energy dissipaters, waterfalls

Dissipaters, zigzag retaining walls.

In urban areas, cement block modules were more appropriate due to the smaller size of the plots and the availability of facilities for manufacturing the construction components.

Adobe is the most appropriate material for Andean highland areas, as there are enough raw materials available and physical access to industrialized materials is difficult, particularly in the highest, steepest or most remote spots. Farmland is required to prepare adobe bricks, which could adversely affect farming activities in poor areas. This limitation should be taken into account in mass housing programmes.

Construction systems

Improved 'quincha' and prefabricated 'quincha' are the basic materials for two construction systems which are adequate for building houses, schools or community buildings, as they can be built quickly and are very earthquake-resilient. Nevertheless, their use depends on the availability of timber resources and skilled manpower and the characteristics of the local climate. A system consistent with local tradition, using improved 'quincha' involves the construction of cane or 'quincha' walls on the construction site itself, making it an efficient use of time and family manpower. Logs and cane of various thicknesses are required. For prefabricated 'quincha', the wood for the panels must be prepared in carpentry workshops and by skilled personnel.

Adobe reinforced with electro-welded mesh is a low-cost alternative for reinforcing existing houses made of basic adobe bricks.

The changes made in the construction of adobe and improved 'quincha' housing during the implementation of Practical Action projects affected the foundations, columns, beams, roof and walls. Concrete was used in the foundations to make them more stable and to protect the walls from damp. In areas with low soil resilience, iron girders were fitted into the foundations and cross-beams to bind the walls. The beams and columns were evenly distributed to ensure the structural resilience of the houses, to which end only one type of material was used, either wood or cement. Plastering the walls with cement improved their resilience to damp and the concrete roof tiles and floor blocks improved the appearance of the homes.

It must be understood that the choice of materials and components should be consistent according to the chosen construction system. The use of a method that has not been tested in a laboratory or that does not abide by building standards should not be promoted.

A workshop was established to manufacture the adobe bricks, cement blocks, roof tiles or other construction components, in an area of at least 50m × 100m, supervised by expert technicians closely involved in the construction work.

Housing designs

When designing the houses, the lifestyles of the project beneficiaries must be borne in mind, taking into consideration that housing modules are used for different purposes depending on the area. Brick and concrete buildings are not only considered to represent higher social status, but they can also extend vertically as the family grows, over a long period of time. On the other hand, rural dwellings are often used to support productive activities, either to store farm crops, breed small animals or set up family vegetable gardens.

The design and concept of the housing must be based on local uses and customs, understanding the priority that people place on using rooms for multiple uses. The houses designed with the beneficiaries not only resulted in a new dwelling that suited their needs, but enabled them to develop their ability to analyse, make suggestions and take decisions for the future.

The following considerations must be borne in mind when designing new architectural models:

- The traditional type of house in the community
- The needs expressed by the beneficiaries participating in the design
- The average area of community plots and the most common dimensions at the front and back of the plots
- The average slope of the land, in order to consider rooms at different levels (terraces, dry-stone walls, etc.)
- The average number of family members
- The distribution of the rooms, based on future water and sewage connections
- Elements like rain, dust, cold, heat.

In the particular case of rural housing, the following should be considered:

- The activities that people use their homes for, other than for living in (e.g. storeroom, crops, garage, breeding of small animals)
- The location of social areas, which are usually at the front of the house
- The kitchen and the bathroom should be next to each other, divided by a wall, in order to save on piping for the water and sewage connections and to minimize the potential for damp in other parts of the house
- The bedrooms should be located at the back of the house, in accordance with the number of people in each family
- Access to the bedrooms, kitchen and bathroom should be through a patio or roofed corridor, depending on the local climate
- There should be a patio at the back of the plot for the breeding of small animals, separate from other daily activities.

According to the experience obtained through Practical Action projects, the most flexible housing design – and consequently the one that has proved the most successful – is a house with two bedrooms and a bathroom fully equipped with water pipes or a septic tank. The architectural design limits the number of openings in the walls and the windows and doors are preferably centred.

Among other aspects, it is necessary to take into account the 'dominant concrete culture' promoted in the communities and accepted by the authorities and by the majority of the urban population.

Other factors to be borne in mind concern potential alternative uses for rooms. In rural areas and in some towns, houses are also used for production purposes, therefore appropriate areas should be planned (for a workshop, shop or storeroom). Housing expansion prospects depend on the area available, therefore in urban areas vertical construction is most feasible.

The construction system designed must improve on the traditional local technology, with a wooden roof covered with tiles.

The designs should reuse traditional shapes like the saddle-type roof, shaped like a cut-off pyramid, which is characteristic of the old buildings in Tacna and Moquegua and well accepted by the beneficiaries in these districts, as it proved adequate for rural houses that tend to expand sideways. However, it is not suitable for densely populated urban areas or plots with topographic limitations where vertical expansion is the only option, unless simpler structures are designed so that the roof can be removed and then rebuilt once the house has been extended.

The technical and economic limitations of the target population must also be taken into account, as the construction of complex roofing requires the services of an expert or the preparation of expensive moulds that are difficult to replicate. In short, it is suggested that the design incorporates a high roof so that the attic can be used as a storeroom and also serve as thermal insulation in both cold and hot climates.

Simple models that can be easily replicated are recommended, flexible enough for beneficiaries to extend or improve their homes in the future.[4]

Administration of the construction work

In reconstruction projects, it is necessary to establish institutional criteria and policies for selecting the beneficiaries and the type of housing assigned to them. The physical characteristics of the people should be taken into account to ensure the work load is allocated appropriately. Weaker people (the sick, the elderly, single mothers, etc.) should be given supporting roles and a specific budget line should be set aside to cover these. The best results were achieved in cases where women participated in the component manufacturing workshops or as construction workers.

In operational terms, a plan of the location of the houses is required, which should be updated during the implementation of the project. The technical files for architectural and engineering projects should be constantly reviewed and improved. Modifications introduced at field level should be incorporated into these as the construction work progresses. It is necessary to have clear forward plans for when the project ends, to be handed over to the authorities and users.

The construction work must be constantly monitored; the quality of the components ensured; the construction itself permanently supervised; and the participants' knowledge of the construction methods continuously reinforced. Throughout the process, random tests on the components manufactured in the workshops must be carried out in order to guarantee a standard quality.

Alliances with government or private programmes should be established to promote and support the production of roof tiles and other prefabricated materials by the victims. This can create income for the participants and encourage replication, where the materials are available locally.

The purchase of materials and equipment, particularly for projects that require a significant number of inputs, should be made locally if possible, to help boost the local economy.

Risk management training

One of the lessons learnt is that risk management training must be included to help improve the community's self-protection, management and organization skills. In rural areas, it may be worth including training in the improvement and protection of infrastructure and agricultural production.

Risk management workshops should try to raise the victims' self-esteem, encouraging them to recognize their rights, skills and relevance in the reconstruction and local development process. The community as a whole should be encouraged to participate in project activities, rather than just the direct beneficiaries of the houses. Links should be established between all the development agents involved to promote the reduction of risk in the reconstruction process. When designing the workshops, consideration should be given both to the main topics and to issues proposed by the population or considered necessary as a result of an analysis of the situation. Such issues might include leadership, gender relations, children's rights, psychological therapy for children and families, parent-child relations, domestic violence, techniques to improve production, small-animal breeding, family vegetable gardens, the history of the community, personal hygiene and cleanliness, food handling, prevention of diseases, community organization and functions, participatory dynamics, protection of river banks, and control of erosion.

Among the main topics covered during the risk management workshops, consideration should be given to: an analysis of the causes of disasters; the roles and responsibilities of organizations and institutions involved in the reconstruction and the identification of their strengths and weaknesses; how to improve community participation and organization; the participatory drafting of risk reduction proposals and plans that include prevention measures; the policies of the different institutions involved; and the mechanisms planned to ensure the participation of the different community organizations.

The main outputs of the workshops are the risk maps in which the population pinpoints the existing threats and vulnerability factors; reconstruction plans and proposals that take into account participatory local development; strategies to disseminate and manage these plans and proposals; and institutional and personal commitments that could affect timelines.

The risk management workshops are mainly directed at the affected adult population, although such workshops can and should also be held with children to encourage good organization among young people. School represents a good alternative to these workshops, in which case emphasis should be placed on the active participation of children, using participatory techniques and dynamics, promoting playful activities, and encouraging creativity through drama, puppets and painting, etc.

Training in construction techniques

Training in construction techniques should take place at the same time as the construction work itself, giving people the skills and capacity to produce materials and carry out the different construction tasks.

The possibility of supporting micro entrepreneurs should be considered, with a view to providing continuity to the production of construction materials and contributing to the workshops.[5]

The organization of child day-care centres for the victims is a helpful mechanism that enables mothers to participate in the training sessions and in the housing construction process whilst their children are protected and looked after.

The following points should be taken into consideration regarding the training in construction technologies:

- The construction process should be linked to the training process. To that end, the construction process should be divided into stages to correspond with the training workshops, e.g. foundations, structural components, roofing, finishing touches, etc.
- When selecting the participants, they should be grouped according to their level of knowledge and education, leadership qualities, commitment and construction know-how. This is a vitally important aspect, as two groups of participants are required: those who have some knowledge of construction, who will lead the replication of the technology to be transferred to the wider population; and those who have no knowledge. The selection

will be based on a very elementary entry test. Gender equality criteria should be factored into the entire process and when children are involved, an age limit should be considered. Instructors must be qualified to make appropriate decisions in this respect.

- When designing the training process, workshops must be defined, minimum content verified, practices established, theoretical lessons planned and a final evaluation conducted. The type and amount of support required for both the theoretical and practical work must also be determined (materials and tools). A schedule of activities must be established as a guideline for supervising them.

- The training must be conducted by a construction technician trained to teach adults. The workshops should include a theoretical part which would preferably take place in a classroom other area set aside for the purpose with appropriate visual aids: videos, flip charts, booklets, standards and/or publications.

The maximum ratio between the trainer and the trainees is 1:20. The teaching materials must be designed for people who can at least read and write. However, appropriate mechanisms should also be designed for illiterate people.

Training in construction should include the following:

- Theoretical sessions covering topics relevant to the construction work. It is advisable to learn the basic concepts and correct implementation of the construction process on site, as it is essential that the structural elements complement each other (e.g. foundations, beams, columns, roofs).

- Practical sessions. The instructor must constantly supervise and guide the work carried out by participants. A basic housing module or community building must be built.

- Evaluation. The only way to measure the level of learning in a training process is by means of ongoing assessments conducted throughout the training process and a final assessment through which the instructor will test participants' level of learning in both theoretical and practical terms.

At the end of the practical activities, the instructor, together with the beneficiaries, will check the planned procedures have been adhered to, the accuracy of the implementation, the quality of the finished products, and how long the construction work took in relation to existing safety conditions. Each participant will sit an examination to test their knowledge of the technology taught, after which a participation certificate will be awarded.

- Certification. Participants who pass the minimum mark will receive a certificate. To this end, it is necessary to work with an institution well known for its role in providing training in construction technologies.

A particular aspect of the training is the need to prioritize improving the skills of local technicians and construction foremen. This training will take longer, but will be remunerated as these trainees will subsequently disseminate the techniques and technologies learnt. Technicians from nearby areas should be included as they will then be able to apply the improved technology in areas outside the project.

Participation

The participation of the affected population is crucial to the success of the reconstruction process. It provides a means of building the houses and of ensuring the continuity of reconstruction processes.

Therefore, projects should obtain the support of existing community organizations from the start, including regarding the selection of beneficiaries, in line with the traditional form of organization derived from self-construction. Families should be encouraged to participate in looking after the children and assign project activities in accordance with the physical capacity of each person. People should be encouraged to design their own homes, help improve their community organizations and carry out collective planning and evaluation activities.

Participation has long-term implications, owing to the individual aptitudes and attitudes it promotes and the effects it has on the group and on the community. Both in Alto Mayo and in Moquegua, the women worked, learnt techniques and took on new roles in the construction process. In addition, based on the knowledge and prestige they obtained through the reconstruction experience and a greater awareness of their capacity and potential, many cast aside their traditional subordinate roles and gradually became leaders of their neighbourhood groups.

Notes

1. For example, during the initial experience in Moquegua, Practical Action-CEOP ILO worked as a consortium fully involved in construction, organization, social promotion and local activities associated with the project. As a result, joint actions were implemented and the project was highly rated.
2. The origins of the weakness of the house in Ayacucho, which could be extrapolated, were caused by the foundations, found to be inadequate in case of earth tremors, and the differential settlement, damp bases, damp caused by capillary action, erosion by rain, beams leaning directly on the walls, deficient plastering and a lack of wall anchors. In this respect, when planning to construct, a soil survey is required to foresee the differential settlement so that a correct scale design can be made and the foundations properly built.
3. Kuroiwa, 2002. The generally accepted method is to: define the study area, carry out on-site geological surveys, obtain historical information, evaluate the area based on the danger level, establishing limits and superimposing all these effects.
4. When designing details like ramps and pavements in Peru, it is necessary to bear in mind Regulation NTE U 190 on Urban Adjustment for disabled people, which regulates the safety of urban and architectural designs. For the structural design, the following Peruvian technical standards must be adhered to regarding the use of timber, cane, 'quincha', adobe and cement blocks:
   - Technical Building Standard NTE E 102 for wooden designs and constructions
   - Ininvi 1982 NTE E 070 for masonry
   - Ininvi NTE E 080 for construction with improved adobe
   - Sencico 2001 primer on the manufacture of and construction with concrete blocks.
5. Business management training is therefore required as well as training in the production of diverse construction materials.

References

Bazant, J. (1983) *Manual de criterios de diseño urbano*, Mexico: Trillas.

Medina, R., and Juvenal (1991) Geodynamic phenomena, study and treatment measures, Lima: Practical Action.

Kuroiwa, J. (2002) *Disaster reduction*, Lima: UNDP.

CHAPTER 5

Guide to the post-disaster intervention method

This chapter contains the proposed 'Guide to the intervention method', based on the lessons learnt through the reconstruction projects and the research work carried out.

The idea is to provide guidelines for community construction projects, establishing an order for the actions and helping those responsible for the process to record and organize the main aspects, bearing in mind complementary actions. The information should be useful when monitoring the progress of the work and making the necessary adjustments that are always required. The forms provided are intended as a starting point and whoever uses them may enhance or improve them.

Reconstruction intervention methodology and guide

Based on the lessons learnt from previous experiences, Practical Action has prepared a methodology and operational guide for the organization of a housing reconstruction process.

The objectives of the guide are as follows: 1) to provide guidelines to professionals and technicians on the adequate and orderly implementation of reconstruction projects applying appropriate technologies; 2) to keep a record of interventions made for monitoring and subsequent evaluation purposes; and 3) to provide professionals and technicians with a long-term evaluation instrument.

The guide can be applied to urban and rural areas, representing the complete history of an intervention from its conception throughout the implementation, completion and monitoring stages. In addition, it contains photographs and videos of beneficiaries and work achieved.

There are four stages in each reconstruction project: 1) the organization and definition of the project; 2) the administration of the construction work; 3) the assessment of beneficiaries; and 4) training and evaluation.

The guide contains forms to be filled in by the project manager or his representative, either by hand or electronically using a Geographical Information System (GIS), for example, so that graphic and alphanumeric data can be correlated. These forms have been validated for the Moquegua III project.

A. Organization and definition of the project

This consists of two forms which contain information on the type of project and its organization, characteristics and scope, in accordance with a preliminary survey of the dangers and needs in the affected area.

The organization and functions refer to the administrative aspects of the project, which provide for decision-making arrangements, flexibility and continuity in the event of unexpected changes. The responsibilities of the participants must be determined (e.g. whether they are acting for one institution in particular or in alliance with other aid agencies), as well as the goals to be achieved. The idea is to obtain answers to the following questions: Who are we going to help and how? Where and in what way? What is the extent and scope of the aid we are giving?

http://dx.doi.org/10.3362/9781780446721.005

Form 1: Organization and functions of participants, administrative staff, professionals and beneficiaries

Form 1 must be filled in with information on the responsibilities and duties assigned to the project participants within the lead institution: administrative staff, professionals and technicians, as well as representatives of the target community, in keeping with the regulation on minimum organization and functions as set out in each institution's 'Manual of administrative standards and procedures', which must be attached to Form 1. It will describe the field of expertise of each participant, how long each one will participate in the project and their decision-making level and responsibility.

Form 2: Preliminary assessment of damage and needs

Form 2 organizes the minimum information required so that the proposal can be based on data that reflect the actual circumstances. One form should be used for each area assessed, in order to record the local variations that appear.

The form will contain information on the area, the number of affected families and the characteristics and extent of the damage suffered by them. This is determined in the field, verifying the type of housing construction, the extent of the damage and the possibility of reusing construction materials from affected buildings.

A survey of the type and level of organization of the population and their capacity to participate will help to define the alliances and institutional aid required. A list must be made of the institutions operating in the area so that formal strategic alliances can eventually be established, including the names of authorities and how to locate them. Information on potential housing reconstruction projects in the area and the location of potential beneficiaries must also be recorded.

Means of access to the area and available means of communication must be taken into consideration.

The natural characteristics and general nature of the land, water sources and predominant construction systems must be described (see Tables 6, 7 and 8 in Chapter 4). Areas that could potentially be used for the workshops and for manufacturing materials will be assessed, as well as the feasibility of employing local resources and local suppliers of inputs and construction equipment.

Mention must be made of the nearest financial institutions to which funds could be transferred for the project managers. Information on the facilities available for the professional and technical staff in charge of implementing the project must be considered, such as food and lodging.

This stage requires general information to be provided regarding the assessment of existing risks, to which end it is worth taking into consideration the guidelines mentioned in the previous chapter, including the characterization of the area according to its topography and climate, context, history of threats, vulnerability, etc.

To prepare this information, it is necessary to obtain information from institutions specializing in geophysical and micro-zoning studies, so that priorities can be established for the intervention in the disaster area. In Peru, the Peruvian Geophysical Institute, IGP, has records of seismic areas, and CISMID specializes in micro seismic-zoning studies. In this respect, the location, quality and characteristics of the land are crucial. Alternatively, it is possible to resort to the procedures mentioned in Chapter 4.

With this survey, the threats, vulnerability and capacities of the local population and of the institutions operating in the area can be assessed.

Based on this information, more appropriate decisions can be taken regarding particular issues to be considered in the reconstruction process.

B. Administration of the construction

The smooth operation of the project depends on the effective technical-administrative monitoring of the works to be implemented. To this end, a complete technical dossier on the construction proposal is required, as well as a schedule for developing the works. The participation of the beneficiaries is required, both in the workshops to manufacture components and in the construction of their homes. Beneficiaries' level of participation, and any difficulties they have or contributions they make, will be detailed on one of the forms.

Forms 3, 4 and 5 contain the technical dossier and the information required to ensure adequate construction and administration.

Form 3: Technical dossier. Architectural plans; structural, sanitary and electrical engineering

This form is the technical dossier, comprising architectural plans, construction details and structural, sanitary and electrical engineering plans. It should contain information on the professionals in charge, the descriptive report, the dimensions of each space and the technical specifications. The technology applied must be consistent with current standards.

Form 4: Administration of the project. Work schedule

This form must contain a list of the work to be implemented and the quantity of materials to be used, estimating how long the implementation will take. Once construction is under way, the actual time taken to complete each piece of work must be mentioned on the second line. If the time taken is longer or shorter than anticipated, the reasons must be indicated in the observations column. This comparison will help control the total project implementation time and enable the project manager to make any necessary adjustments.

Form 5: Workshop to manufacture construction components

Form 5 registers the types of construction components to be produced in the workshop, the different stages of production, including the start date and end date, and the number of participants by gender, age (including children and the elderly) and disability status. The names and ages of the participants and a photograph of the workshop will be included.

C. Assessment of beneficiaries

In order to ensure an appropriate selection of beneficiaries, the most vulnerable people must be identified by means of a survey which examines the socio-economic situation of the families, their physical situation and the legal status of the properties to be rebuilt. Forms 6, 7 and 8 are used for this purpose.

Form 6: Qualification for receiving benefits

In order to select the beneficiaries, the actual needs of the affected families must be identified. One member of each family will be listed as the head of the household, together with details of their address, occupation, level of participation in the community, family structure, access to health infrastructure, socio-economic situation, physical situation and legal status of their property, plus a few observations made by the assessor. Giving the actual circumstances in which many potential beneficiaries in rural areas live, undocumented people will not be excluded from list of potential beneficiaries. Any resources (e.g. construction materials) that might be recovered from the homes will also be assessed, and the form will also mention any benefits or difficulties that could arise in an eventual intervention, as well as any aid that might be received from other institutions, in order to avoid duplication. Finally, the assessor must decide whether or not some kind of benefit should be granted.

Form 7: Location of the beneficiaries and type of housing

On the map showing the location of the houses in the area, the most prominent reference points must be mentioned: street names, bridges, rivers, geographical features, number of blocks, lots or plots, or any other reference to pinpoint their correct location. A list of beneficiaries, the name of the head of the household and the type of housing planned for them must be included.

Form 8: Project monitoring

Form 8 contains a photograph of the destroyed house and the beneficiary family, mentioning the date it was taken. The state of the house and the characteristics of its location must be mentioned. When the reconstruction is completed, a photograph of the beneficiary family in front of the new house must be added, mentioning the delivery date. In addition, a space is provided on the form for evaluating the results of the project, and the situation of the house, and any modifications to it, after it has been used for 'x' years.

D. Training

Training in risk management and construction technologies is provided as part of the project. To this end, the participants must be selected according to their skills, knowledge and previous experience in construction work. Once the reconstruction is completed, a certificate will be awarded.

For construction training, an organized work plan detailing the people responsible and the materials used, is are established during the workshops. Forms 9, 10 and 11 should be used to support this.

Form 9: Training process: entry test, final test

Participants are identified based on their level of knowledge and general education, particularly in terms of their knowledge of construction work. Two groups of participants are required: 1) those who have knowledge of construction work, who will replicate the technology in the future; and 2) those who have no knowledge of construction work, who will be taught construction skills so that they will be qualified as skilled manpower for basic tasks that will enable them to support the construction work. The selection is based on a very elementary entry test, which will be adjusted according to the system to be implemented. When participants complete the reconstruction project, they will be tested on the techniques applied in order to refresh their memory, after which they will receive a participation certificate or, eventually, a certification.

Form 10: Training modules

This form includes details of the number and scope of training workshops, their core content, the practical work, theoretical lessons and assessments, and lists of participants. A construction technician or a risk management expert will be in charge of each training module. The training modules on construction technologies will contain a theoretical part which will take place in a suitable place with visual aids as considered necessary: appropriate videos, flip charts, booklets, standards or publications. For the practical work, the instructor will take the group to the demonstration construction site, with enough tools and appropriate good quality equipment for all participants.

Assessments are the best way to gauge the level of learning achieved through a training process, therefore there will be continuous assessment throughout the training and construction processes. Depending on the results obtained, the lead institution will award a certificate to the beneficiaries who obtain a pass mark.

Form 11: Summary of the intervention methodology

Finally, form 11 summarizes all the forms and documents that comprise the history of the project, in correlative order. Minutes of agreements, and of the final acceptance of the whole project's completion by each beneficiary, will be attached as annexes.

Guide to the Intervention Method

ORGANIZATION & DEFINITION OF THE PROJECT	ADMINISTRATION OF THE CONSTRUCTION WORK	CHARACTERIZATION OF BENEFICIARIES	TRAINING AND EVALUATION
Form 1 ORGANIZATION AND DUTIES of participants, administrative staff, professionals and beneficiaries	Form 3 TECHNICAL DOSSIER Architecture, structures, sanitary and electrical fixtures plans, responsible professionals, descriptive reports, estimated measurements	Form 6 QUALIFICATION FOR RECEIVING BENEFITS Data on head of household, family structure, physical and socio-economic situation, legal status, aid received.	Form 9 TRAINING PROCESS Entry test for participating beneficiaries
Form 2 PRELIMINARY EVALUATION OF DAMAGES, NEEDS AND RISKS Evaluation of damages and conditions for establishing a reconstruction or similar programme. Micro seismic zoning, history of hazards, environmental problems.	Form 4 ADMINISTRATION OF THE PROJECT – WORK SCHEDULE Progress of the project, works and disbursements.	Form 7 LOCATION OF BENEFICIARIES Map of the city pinpointing the location of each beneficiary and the type of housing	Form 10 APPLICATION OF THE TRAINING SESSIONS
	Form 5 COMPONENT MANUFACTURING WORKSHOPS Participants and organization	Form 8 PROJECT MONITORING Photographic file: Initial and final state of each beneficiary's house	Form 11 SUMMARY OF THE INTERVENTION METHODOLOGY

FORM 1: ORGANIZATION AND FUNCTIONS OF PARTICIPANTS, ADMINISTRATIVE STAFF, PROFESSIONALS AND BENEFICIARIES

Project:

Type of event

Area of event[1]

Role of participating agents		Name	Responsibilities	Participation schedule[2]										Date[4]	
Role	Field of expertise			1	2	3	4	5	6	7	8	9	10	Start	End
Project Manager															
Administration staff	Permanent[3]														
	Temporary														
Risk management experts[5]	Permanent														
	Temporary														
Construction experts	Architect														
	Civil engineer														
	Electrical engineer														
	Sanitary engineer														
	Others														
Construction and training technicians	Technician 1														
	Technician 2														
	Technician 3														
	Technician 4														
	Technician 5														
Community	Community leader 1														
	Community leader 2														
	Community leader 3														
	Community leader 4														

Practical Action Intervention Methodology. First review: February 2004

NOTES FOR FILLING IN THE FORM:
1. Refers to the nearest community
2. In weeks or months, depending on the duration of the project
3. Draw bar graphs to indicate number of weeks or months required
4. The date refers to the length of participation in the project
5. Name, professional expertise and characteristics of their contract

FORM 2: PRELIMINARY EVALUATION OF DAMAGES AND RISKS

1. Person responsible				
2. Evaluation date				
3. Evaluation of damage: number of homes destroyed				
Recovery of materials	All	Part	None	Observations
4. Number of families affected				
Number	% of the total			
Characteristics of the families				
Level of damage				
Specific needs of women and children				

5. Local organization	Operating in the area	Information available	Is there a relo-cation area?
President of the Region	Yes/No	Yes/No	Yes/No
Mayor (provincial, district or delegation)	Yes/No	Yes/No	Yes/No
President of the Community	Yes/No	Yes/No	Yes/No
Observations regarding participation and organization problems			

Date identified	Address	Telephone	E-mail

6. Institutions operating in the area	
Name	Objective

Area of the event	
Type of event	
11. Building systems used in the area	Description
12. Areas available for	
Workshops	Yes/No
Recovery zone	
Storage of materials and equipment	

13. Availability of local resources		Volume
Farm soil		Sufficient/insufficient
Reed, cane, straw		Sufficient/insufficient
Aggregates	Sand	Sufficient/insufficient
	Gravel	Sufficient/insufficient
	Crushed stone	Sufficient/insufficient

14. Suppliers of construction materials and equipment
Existent
Formal
Type of materials
Cement
Construction iron

7. Means of access and time/distance from the district capital

On foot		
By road	Paved	Track
By river	Boat	Canoe	Barge	Ship
By air		

8. Means of communication (radio, telephone, mobile, internet):

State of roads	Description, feasibility and frequency of use

Aggregates
Timber

Equipment suppliers:

Local institutions
Private institutions

15. Feasibility of transferring funds:

Banks	Yes/No

16. Lodging	Address, telephone, reference
Food	Address, telephone, reference

17. State of the population	Institutions operating
Quality	Situation perceived

9. General characteristics of the land

Nature of the land	Flat	Undulating	Sloping
	Sandy	Clayey	Rocky

10. Water sources (Indicate availability per day, or permanent)

Rural	Quality	Time	Quality
Spring	Cistern		
River	Well		
Well	Tank		
Canal	Reservoir		
Other	Public network		

Instructions for filling in the form:

Specify the location and the estimated number of families and houses affected, in numerical and percentage terms. This must be determined in the field, where it is also necessary to identify the construction system used, the characteristics of the families, how badly they were affected and the specific needs of the women, children and the most vulnerable population.

Recognizing the level and type of local organization will help to establish alliances and institutional assistance. The institutions operating in the area must also be listed so that formal strategic alliances can eventually be established. To describe the natural characteristics and general nature of the land, use tables 6, 7 and 8, means and types of access to the area and their state, specifying particular characteristics in terms of difficulty and frequency of use. In many areas where access is difficult, certain days, times and one-way use of the roads have been established locally, which must be taken into consideration so as not to affect the supply of the staff, equipment and inputs required. With a view to implementing the reconstruction project, existing local materials and suppliers of construction materials must be defined, including the estimated volumes available.

The evaluator should give his/her opinion on the situation of the families, community organization and the relationship between existing organizations. It would be advisable to include photos taken during the preliminary evaluation. Consideration must be given to minimum initial facilities for the staff implementing the project, such as food and lodging.

Person responsible:

Map of the city, community, settlement, others in UTM coordinates, with contour lines every metre.

		NAME OF THE AREA/COMMUNITY
Date:	Area of the event	
		Community President:
Urban plans		Region
		Provincial municipality
		District municipality
	Micro seismic zoning	
History of hazards		Chronology, location
Environmental problems		Degradation, lack of natural resources
Risk areas		Alluvial fans
		Landslide areas
		Level of water tables
		Others
Reconstruction		In the same place
		Within their own property
		In municipal or community land*
Relocation		Redevelopment
Infrastructure		Water
		Sewage
		Energy
Complementary works		Environment – landscape
Observations		
Local Organizations		

*Agreements, acceptance certificates

FORM 3.1: ARCHITECTURAL TECHNICAL DOSSIER

Project	Project name
	Name of the community
Area of the event	
Professional responsible for the reconstruction project	
ARCHITECTURAL TYPOLOGY	
Architectural plan: floor plan, first floor, roof	Architectural plan: shears and elevations
	Architectural plan: perspectives and details
DESCRIPTIVE REPORT	
	Map of the location in the community
Location	Professional responsible for the project
	Name and signature
Concept	
	Association number
Uses	
	Observations
Details	

FORM 3.2: STRUCTURAL TECHNICAL DOSSIER

Project	Project name
Area of the event	Name of the community
Professional responsible for the reconstruction project	Professional responsible for the project

ARCHITECTURAL TYPOLOGY

Structural plan: showing foundation, walls and columns, roofing	Structural plan: construction details	Name and signature
		Association number Date
		Descriptive Report

Summary of estimated measurements		Cement	Iron	Timber	Adobe	Cement blocks	Aggregates m²	Roof tiles	Façade	Paint	Budget	US$/ Euros
Item	Unit	Bags				Wall	Thick sand		Doors		Total amount	
	Estimated measurementss					Floor	Small stones		Windows			
							Concrete					
1	Walls m²										Services	
2	Columns units										Materials	
3	Staircase unit										Total services	
4	Roof m²										Roof and covering	
5	Plaster m²										Walls and plaster	
	Sub total										Technical assistance	
	Existing beneficiary material										US$ = X S/.	
	Material to be purchased											
	Highest price											
	Amount requested											

FORM 3.3: SANITARY FIXTURES TECHNICAL DOSSIER SANITARY ENGINEERING

Project	Project name
Area of the event	Name of the community
Professional responsible for the reconstruction project	
ARCHITECTURAL TYPOLOGY	

Plan of sanitary facilities: water plant, details	Plan of sanitary facilities: Sewage plant, details
	Professional responsible for the project
	Name and signature
	Association number Date
	Descriptive Report

Summary of estimated measurements

Item	Size	Description
Sewage pipes		
Sewage pipes		
Water pipes		
Water pipes		
Accessories		
Toilet		
Washbasin		
Shower		

FORM 3.4: ELECTRICAL INSTALLATIONS TECHNICAL DOSSIER ELECTRICAL ENGINEERING

Project	Project name	
Area of the event	Name of the community	
Professional responsible for the reconstruction project		
ARCHITECTURAL TYPOLOGY		
Plan of electrical facilities: installation plant, details	Plan of electrical installations, details	Professional responsible for the project
		Name and signature
		Association number — Date
		Descriptive Report
		Summary of estimated measurements

Item	Size	Description
Plugs		
Switches		
No. Cables		
No. Cables		
Accessories		
Other		

FORM 4: ADMINISTRATION OF THE PROJECT – Work Schedule

Project

Location

Professional responsible

Starting date

Work progress schedule

Items	1		2	3	4	5	6	Observations
	1–30 days		31–60 days	61–90 days	91–120 days	121–150 days	151–180 days	
		Proposed schedule						
		Actual schedule						

Instructions for filling in the form

The work schedule is applied to the entire project during the planning stage, in order to anticipate the time spans required.

Progress of the works: draw up a list of the anticipated items in accordance with the type of project and the estimated implementation time, with horizontal bars indicating the graphical sequence, so that the progress and timing of the works can be appreciated.

Observations: In the event of any changes in the terms or the items, specify the reasons.

FORM 5: WORKSHOPS TO MANUFACTURE CONSTRUCTION COMPONENTS

Project

Location

Person responsible

Workshop

No.	Product[1]	Date		Participants[2]		Observations[3]
		Starting date	End date	Number		
1	Adobe				Men	
					Women	
					Children	
					Others	
2	Cement blocks				Men	
					Women	
					Children	
					Others	
3	Quincha panels				Men	
					Women	
					Children	
					Others	
4	Steel work				Men	
					Women	
					Children	
					Others	
5	Roof trusses				Men	
					Women	
					Children	
					Others	
6	Roof tiles				Men	
					Women	

		Children			
		Others			
7	Floors	Men			
		Women			
		Children			
		Others			
8	Others	Men			
		Women			
		Children			
		Others			

Photograph of the workshop

Participants	
Name and age[4]	
1	
2	
3	
4	
etc.	

Notes:
1. Type of components required for each workshop
2. Number and characteristics of participants: men, women, children, disabled, elderly
3. Strengths and weaknesses of workshop participants
4. Full names and ages of all participants

FORM 6: QUALIFICATION FOR OBTAINING THE BENEFIT

Project: Name of the project

Type of event:

Area of the event: Name of the community

1 Data on the Head of Household

Occupation		
Surnames		Name
I.D. No.		No documents
Civil status		Male/Female
Urban area: Job situation		
Rural area: Farming, cattle-raising, fishing, others		
Owner, contractor, day labourer		

Participation in the community

Leader	Community member	Inhabitant	Tenant	Others
State of health	Good	Average	Bad	Disabled	Others

2 Family Structure[1]

Name	Relationship	Age	Civil Status	Occupation		Description
				Urban area	Rural area	

3 Situation of the inhabitants of the plot

Situation of the family[2]

Sanitation	Water	Well/drought	Public Network	Sanitary facilities	Public sewerage	Septic tank/others

Socio-Economic Situation[3]

Number of families living on the plot

Number of habitable rooms

Number of dependents living together | Adults | Children

4 Tick their possessions

Kitchen stove	Vehicles	Tools	Refrigerator	Radio / TV	Cattle/small animals	Crops	Tools

5 Aid Received[4]

Housing module, construction material, tent, warm clothing, food

Specify

6 Physical-legal clearance

6.1 Location

Area	Urban	Block	Plot	Rural	Property	Plot

Ownership document

6.2

Title deed (specify the public entity that awarded it)		COFOPRI title deed	Code
Purchase – Sale Contract		Others	
Possession/award certificate		Specify	

Characteristics of the plot[5]

Area of the plot

6.3

Situation	Destroyed	Slightly damaged	Seriously damaged	Very seriously damaged	Description
Not built					
Construction in process	Predominant material	Roofing	Light/precarious		

6.4 Domestic connections – access to services

Water	Sewage	Electricity	Telephone	Recoverable material

6.5

Land				
Soil	**State**	**Type**	**State**	**Type**
Flat		Brick		Timber
Characteristic slopes		Cement blocks		Cane
Hillside		Adobe		Zinc sheeting
Risk area		Precarious		Ichu
Alluvial fan		Compact earth		Provisional
Others, specify		Others		Others

Owner / beneficiary	Signature
Evaluator's observations	
Mark:[6]	
Evaluator's name	Date

INSTRUCTIONS FOR FILLING IN THE FORM

1. List all family members
2. Family situation after the disaster
3. Relevance of the benefit to be received
4. To be ticked if aid was received.
5. Summarize the situation of the plot in terms of need and the reconstruction potential
6. Benefit qualification mark awarded by the evaluator

FORM 7: LOCATION OF BENEFICIARIES AND TYPE OF HOUSING

Project:	Name of the project
Person responsible:	
Type of event:	
Area of the event	Name of the community
References:	President of the community

Plan of the city, community, settlement, others, in coordinates UTM, with contour line every metre. Source: NGI (example)

Beneficiary population

	Name	Type of module	Address
1			
2			
3			
4			
etc.			

FORM 8. PROJECT MONITORING

Project	Name of the project
Location	
Professional responsible:	
Name of the owner – beneficiary	

Photo of the initial state	Photo of the destroyed house

Monitoring: Photograph of the site after x years with the resident and family

Photo of the final state	Photo of the rebuilt house

		Date
Observations		
Person responsible for the evaluation		

FORM 9. TRAINING PROCESS – Entry Test

Project	Name of the project															
Area of the event	Name of the community															
Professional evaluator																
Name	Name of the beneficiary															
PART I[1]	Basic knowledge	Mark														
1.	Elementary operations	Addition, subtraction, multiplication and division														
	Addition															
	Subtraction															
	Multiplication															
	Division															
2.	Basic knowledge of the decimal metric system															
	mm															
	cm															
	metre															
3.	Knowledge of lineal, area and volume measurements															
	m															
	m²															
	m³															
PART II[2]	Physical aptitude	Carrying capacity and correct posture														
1.	Carrying between 10 and 15 kilos of weight															
2.	Carrying between 15 and 20 kilos of weight															
3.	Carrying between 20 and 30 kilos of weight															
4.	Pushing a loaded wheelbarrow or buggy															
PART III[3]	Basic knowledge of construction work															
1.	Reading plans															
2.	Measuring															
3.	Running a level															
4.	Using a plumb bob															

5.	Drawing with a set square									
6.	Mixing mud									
7.	Mixing cement and sand									
8.	Others									
PART IV[4]	Risk management									
1.	Knowledge of assembly procedures									
2.	Knowledge of housing locations									
3.	Knowledge of causes of disasters									
4.	Knowledge of mitigation measures									
5.	Knowledge of responsibilities for dealing with risks									
6.	Knowledge of civil defence									
7.	Knowledge of organization of task forces									
	Overall mark[5]									

Instructions for filling in the form:
1. Evaluate the beneficiary's mathematical skills
2. Evaluate the beneficiary's physical capacity for construction work
3. Evaluate the knowledge of construction required to qualify the beneficiary
4. Evaluate the beneficiary's basic knowledge of risk management
5. Classification of the beneficiary within the construction activities.

FORM 9.1 TRAINING PROCESS: Final Test

Final test: QUINCHA

Project:	Name of the project
Area of the event	Name of the community
Professional evaluator	
Name	Name of beneficiary
Brief answers:	
1	Draw a sketch of the wooden frames to be used for building with quincha
2	Explain what the plaited cane in the quincha panels consists of
3	Explain how the quincha panels are fitted onto the footings
4	Describe how the mud is prepared to cover the quincha. Primary plastering
5	Explain how the final mix is prepared to plaster the walls of the quincha module
6	What is a burnisher and where is it applied?
7	Describe how the mix for the foundation of a quincha construction is prepared, its dimensions and the materials employed
8	Explain how the panels are assembled and how they are joined together
9	What is a roof beam and what is it for?
10	Explain the system used to protect the wood used in the construction, where and how it is applied
	.... Mark:
RECOMMENDATIONS FOR THE EVALUATOR	
Emphasis should be placed on carpentry aspects, the mud preparation and the assembly	
The questions should be read out and explained to the students before they proceed to answer them	
When marking the tests, priority should be placed on the knowledge rather than on the form of expression	
It is recommended that the pass rate should be 70% or more.	

FORM 9.2 TRAINING PROCESS: Final Test

Final test: IMPROVED ADOBE

Project:	Name of the project
Area of the event	Name of the community
Name of beneficiary	
Brief answers:	
1	What materials are used to make adobes?
2	What are the correct measurements of an adobe?
3	Describe how to prepare the mud for making adobes
4	Describe the way the adobes are moulded
5	How are the adobes stored once they are made and how long must they be left to dry before using them?
6	Describe how to prepare the mix for an adobe construction and what materials are employed
7	How many rows of adobes can be made per day and after how many rows is a horizontal reinforcement required?
8	What is the ring beam and what is it for?
9	How far should the roof or covering go beyond the wall?
10	How many layers of plaster are applied to an adobe wall and what material is used?
	.... Mark:
RECOMMENDATIONS FOR THE EVALUATOR	
	For adobe constructions, emphasis should be placed on preparing the mud and making the adobes
	The questions should be read out and explained to the students before they proceed to answer them
	When marking the tests, priority should be placed on the knowledge rather than on the form of expression
	It is recommended that the pass rate should be 70% or more.

FORM 9.3 TRAINING PROCESS: Final Test

Final test: CONCRETE BLOCKS

Project:	Name of the project
Area of the event	Name of the community
Professional evaluator	
Name	Name of beneficiary
1	Mention all the types of blocks used in the construction process and what they are used for
2	Briefly explain what aggregates are, the dosage of the mixture, what a mould is, how the blocks are cured and how the quality of the concrete blocks is controlled
3	Indicate the proportion of materials mixed to prepare the concrete blocks
4	Describe how the blocks are moulded
5	What precautions should be taken to make sure the concrete blocks set?
6	What is the main characteristic of reinforced masonry construction?
7	What is the maximum daily progress when building a concrete block wall?
8	Explain how the vertical reinforcement bars are fixed into the concrete
9	What is an adit?
10	Explain what the "U" blocks are used for and how the roof beam is built
	.... Mark:
	RECOMMENDATIONS FOR THE EVALUATOR
	Emphasis should be placed on the block manufacturing aspects, building the walls and fitting in the reinforcements
	The questions should be read out and explained to the students before they proceed to answer them
	When marking the tests, priority should be placed on the knowledge rather than on the form of expression
	It is recommended that the pass rate should be 70% or more.

FORM 9.4 TRAINING PROCESS: Final Test

Final test: RISK MANAGEMENT

Project:	Name of the project
Area of the event	Name of the community
Name	
Brief answers	Name of beneficiary
1	What is the difference between threat and vulnerability?
2	What measures may be useful for reducing risks?
3	In what way is the community capable of reducing risks?
4	Which institutions and authorities are responsible for dealing with risks and disasters?
5	Who should participate in assemblies?
6	Which land should not be used to build houses?
7	Which are the main disaster risks in the community?
8	How can we protect our crops and animals from disasters?
	How can we protect our homes from disasters?
9	What are the responsibilities of the municipality in terms of reducing disaster risks in our community?
	What are our own responsibilities for reducing disaster risks and how?
	What organizations should work to prevent disasters and how?
10	Who forms part of the civil defence?
	How can we participate in civil defence?
11	How can we improve organization in our community?
	.... Mark:
	RECOMMENDATIONS FOR THE EVALUATOR
	The questions should be read out and explained to the students before they proceed to answer them
	When marking the tests, priority should be placed on the knowledge rather than on the form of expression
	It is recommended that the pass rate should be 70% or more.

FORM 10: TRAINING APPLICATION

Project:	Name of the project
Area of the event	Name of the community
Instructor responsible	

	Workshop	Contents	Hours	Instructor	Teaching material	Date	Participants	Observations
Construction process and training workshops	First	Technical presentation, materials, foundation						
	Second	Technical presentation						
	Third	Practical demonstration						
	Fourth	Practical demonstration						
	Fifth	Practical demonstration						
	Sixth	Others						
	Seventh							

	Type of workshop	Materials workshops	Hours	Instructor	Teaching material	Date	Participants	Observations
Implementation of the training sessions	Cement blocks	Production						
		Mix preparation, unmoulding, curing						
	Iron	Cutting, bending, abutting, others						
	Adobe	Preparation, moulding, piling, drying, placing on the site						
	Windows	Preparation, cutting, conditioning, installing, finishing						
	Roof tiles	Production, preparing the mix, distribution, curing						
	Others							
	Others							

	Type of workshop	Materials workshops	Hours	Instructor	Teaching material	Date	Participants	Observations
	Foundation	Levelling, layout, excavation, placing columns, filling						
	Columns	Placing, levelling, filling, removing formwork						
	Walls	Setting, levelling, finishing						
	Roofs	Stages relevant to the type of roof						
	Others							
	Workshop	Risk management						
	First	Introduction: traditional approach and risk management						
	Second	Risks and their components: threats, vulnerabilities, capabilities						
	Third	Risk evaluations and local plans						
Risk Management	Fourth	Institutions and risk management						
	Fifth	Organization and risk management						
	Sixth	Risk-related rights and responsibilities						
	Seventh	Community participation and risk management						
	Eighth	Evaluation of the reconstruction experience						

FORM 11: SUMMARY OF THE INTERVENTION METHODOLOGY

	Description	Information	Observations
Form 1: ORGANIZATION AND FUNCTIONS Policies, organization chart, decision flow charts, responsibilities	Responsibilities: attributes of each project participant and their decision-making levels	OFR: Organization and Functions Regulations	Practical Action – ITDG Handbook of Standards and Procedures
	Organization chart showing the position and duties of team members	Management, coordination, headquarters, professionals responsible for work plans or specific studies, training technicians, assistant technicians	Avoids confusion and conflicts when making decisions
	Policy to be followed: framework of disaster programmes	Establishes the institutional framework that upholds the project, which must be borne in mind and used as a reference in the event of any doubts and to avoid any deviation from the objective	Define whether the project includes training and if so, the cost of the training.
	Decisions: channelling queries	How to communicate and transmit decisions taken to implement the project, organization sequence and organization chart	How and over which periods of time?
Form 2: PRELIMINARY EVALUATION OF DAMAGES, NEEDS AND RISKS	General information	Damages and conditions for establishing a re-construction or similar programme, local organizations	Probable number of victims, photographic file of the area, operational information
		History of the area, history of hazards	Brief account of the background affecting the project
		Existing population statistics	INEI and others
	Specific information	Geographical location, topography	Location of the working area referring to official sources (NGI), basic description and meteorological characteristics
		Environmental problems	Degradation, natural resources
		Location of the city and location of the intervention, type of event	Survey of the situation and elements to be taken into consideration
		Seasonal aspects affecting the works (rain, winds, harvests, etc.)	Demolition, land clearance
			To be considered in the works programme
	Existing conditions	Local identity (culture)	Urban values and type of architecture
		Urban-spatial	Settlement patterns, size and shape of plots
		Sanitation and electricity services	Existing services and quality
			Identification of the EAP involved in construction, existing technology, possible applications, improvements
		Construction technology	Proposed type of construction

Form	Item	Detail
Form 3: TECHNICAL DOSSIER. ARCHITECTURE, STRUCTURES, ELECTRICAL INSTALLATIONS, SANITARY FACILITIES	Work plan	Scale model of the project: in detail
	Laboratory tests	Calculator's approval, laboratory certificates
	Plans	Detailed scale model of the project
	Specifications and recommendations	Existing handbooks
	Construction system: conventional and/or with technological innovation	Use the well-known technology and local technicians as temporary manpower
	Experience of local construction technicians	Work plans, technical specifications, in accordance with current national standards
	Management and construction responsibility	Verification by the project manager, in accordance with the specifications and/or current standards
	Professional technical assistance method	Stages of the intervention and responsibilities
	Approval of the quality of materials	
	Professionals involved	
Form 4: ADMINISTRATION OF THE PROJECT – WORK SCHEDULE	Preliminary schedule	Works monitoring
	List of items vs. implementation plan	Financial monitoring
	Disbursements schedule	
	Purchases and payments	Depending on the type of material and level of formality
	Orders, requests, cheques, cash	In the project office and in the main office
	Accounting system, record of disbursements	If no valid documents are available, with the authorization of the project manager
	Register of purchases and payments	
	Determine the scale of disbursements with no vouchers	
	Persons responsible	According to the organization chart
Form 5: ADMINISTRATION OF THE CONSTRUCTION – WORKSHOPS TO MANUFACTURE CONSTRUCTION COMPONENTS	Administration and distribution	
	Production plant and warehouse	Land use agreement or authorization, inventory of machinery, tools and inputs
	Cost	Compared with the budgets
	Preliminary control	Establish production goals by weeks, months
	Delivery control	Acceptance by beneficiaries or users
	Evaluation of alliances with similar producers in the area	Provide continuity to the workshop
	Cost – benefit	

Form			
	Social organization	Community, association, cooperative, others	Name of the President, number of members
	Preliminary estimates of local applicants	According to relevant institutions	Field data of INDECI, other NGOs
		According to field estimates	Verification
	Social	Social identity, local leaders	Describe the organization and local values
		Socio-economic	Describe the initial situation, income, the situation of widows, the disabled and others
		Gender	Number, age
		Family burden	Dependents, young families
		Economic capacity	Unemployed EAP
Form 6: QUALIFICATION FOR OBTAINING THE BENEFIT		Type of land possession	Typology of the home assigned to the beneficiary
		Criteria and exceptions	Community decisions
	Formal	In urban area through a selection in the field	Random checking of data
		In rural area at community assemblies	Random checking of data
	Selection of beneficiaries	Scale map with topographic lines, blocks, names of neighbourhoods, streets, plots, references and location of types of urban equipment, houses built and names of their owners, keys and graphic scale	Organize in electronic and printed forms
Form 7: LOCATION OF BENEFICIARIES AND TYPE OF HOUSING	Town, including the location and name of each beneficiary	Photographs of the initial condition before the work, photograph of the delivery of the house and photograph after x years for evaluation purposes	Comments on the situation, changes and modifications, observations regarding the performance of the technology used, comments on the beneficiary's personal situation
Form 8: PROJECT MONITORING	Photographic file on each house built by the project	Elementary entry test and minimum score	Identification of local leaders, previous experience in construction. Quantification of the economic effect of the training on the cost of the works
Form 9: TRAINING PROCESS – Entry test – final test	Selection of participants	Characterization of the beneficiary participating in the construction	Two groups of participants, those with previous knowledge and unskilled labourers
Form 10: APPLICATION OF THE TRAINING SESSIONS	Design of the construction process by stages corresponding to the training modules	Definition and contents of the modules	Handbooks, scale models, cost and potential replication, preparation of local technicians as "extension workers"
	Implementation of the training sessions	Training workshops, application of lessons obtained	Participation consistency
Form 11: SUMMARY OF THE INTERVENTION METHODOLOGY	Compilation of all previous forms and minutes	In the project records, the forms are compiled in chronological order and attached as appendices to the minutes of agreements and of the final delivery of the project as a whole and for each beneficiary	

The description of the phases does not include the entire administrative design, only the part that the institution has already implemented should be included. All the forms will be filed in electronic and printed forms.

ANNEX

Annex 1.1 Risk-zoning studies and maps

The Risk Map provided the necessary tool for locating, controlling, monitoring and representing in graphic form the risk generating agents that cause occupational accidents or workplace-related diseases. It has been systematized and adjusted in order to create and maintain safe working environments and conditions for workers, so that they can perform better in their jobs and preserve their health.

The term Risk Map is relatively new and originated in Europe, specifically in Italy, towards the end of the sixties, as part of the strategy adopted by Italian trade unions to protect the health of the working population.

Risk assessment

In this process, the factors that create risk are assessed by means of measuring techniques recommended in national and international standards, complemented by the application of the following mechanisms and techniques:

A methodology to determine the nature and extent of the risk by analyzing potential hazards and evaluating existing vulnerability factors that represent a potential threat or could cause harm to the population and the properties, livelihoods and environment they depend on.

The risk assessment process is based on a review of the technical characteristics of the threats, i.e. their location, magnitude or intensity, frequency and probability, as well as an analysis of the physical, social, economic and environmental dimensions of the vulnerability and exposure, giving special consideration to the capacity available to deal with the different risk scenarios.

Drawing up the map

Based on the identification and assessment of the factors that generate local risks, the information compiled is analysed to reach conclusions and propose improvements; these are then represented in different kinds of tables and in graphic form in a Risk Map, using relevant symbols.

The Risk Map consists of a graphic representation containing generally used or adopted symbols, indicating level of exposure – low, medium or high – in accordance with the information compiled in files and the measurements taken of existing risk factors; this makes it easier to control and monitor them by implementing prevention programmes.

The schedule for drawing up the Risk Map is based on the following factors:

- Depending on the geographical area to be considered in the study, the Risk Map can be applied to large areas such as countries or states, or to smaller scale areas such as districts, cities, neighbourhoods or communities, and even institutional and/or residential sites.
- Selection of the area: This consists of defining the geographical area to be considered in the study and the issues to be dealt with there.
- Collecting information: During this stage, historical and operational documentation on the selected geographical area is gathered, including information on the people who work there and existing prevention plans.

http://dx.doi.org/10.3362/9781780446721.006

Also, the time period for which the risk factors apply should be based on actual data; otherwise the date of the beginning of the study.

Identification of risks: through this process, risk generating agents are identified. Below are some of the methods used to obtain information:

- Opinion polls: obtaining information from workers through surveys on occupational hazards and working conditions
- Checklist: a list of possible risks that could be encountered in a specific working environment
- Danger index: a checklist ranking the risks identified in order of their danger level.

Annex 1.2 Analysis of the construction designs and experiences of different institutions

This annex describes the experiences and research work of the Disaster Prevention and Study Centre (Predes), the material-testing laboratories of the Pontificate Catholic University of Peru, and the Programme to Support Repopulation and Development in emergency areas (PAR), involving improved and prefabricated 'quincha', adobe reinforced with electro-welded mesh and earthquake-resilient adobe constructions.

These experiences were selected because the use of materials, components and appropriate technology are common denominators, in view of the need for them to be more earthquake-resilient and respond to local geographical characteristics. Other common factors are the target population and the community-based search for practical construction practices.

The following records describe the negotiating or implementing entities, the type of financing, the number of houses built, the built-up areas and the unit cost in US dollars. In terms of the project, details are provided of the location and geographical surroundings, existing infrastructure (if any) and the model for the houses built, as well as information regarding the participation of the population and the results achieved with regard to the advantages and limitations of the systems employed.

IMPROVED 'QUINCHA'

Negotiating and implementing entity
Disaster Prevention and Study Centre (Predes) and the Italian Cooperation Agency (COOPI)

Financing
European Commission Humanitarian Aid Office (ECHO)

Place
District municipalities of Cocachacra, Aplao, Huancarqui and Corire, in the district of Arequipa.

Number of houses
300 housing modules

Area of each house
24 m^2

Cost per module
US$1,089.33

Module under construction

Finished module housing

Date
September and October 2001

Advantages
Due to its thermal qualities, 'quincha' adapted well to the local climate conditions. It is cool both during the day and at night; in addition, since local materials are used, the buildings are easily adaptable to the local environment.

Limitations
The cane is susceptible to rotting when exposed; therefore it needs to be adequately treated.

IMPROVED 'QUINCHA' – PREDES

LOCATION AND SURROUNDINGS

The project was located in the middle of the Majes watershed and the lower Tambo river basin, in areas between 450 and 700m above sea level and between 100 and 250m above sea level.

The climate in these areas is hot and dry, with predominantly high temperatures, this being a desert area. Strong winds blow in the afternoons. The rainy season is from December to March, although the rainfall is negligible.

The land is fairly irregular, slightly undulating with few or medium slopes. The bearing capacity of the soil is 0.5 kg/cm^2.

EXISTING INFRASTRUCTURE

Water: Although there was a water supply system, it could not meet the existing demand, except in Carrizal on the Tambo river.

Sewage: There was neither a sewage network nor any excreta disposal system.

Electricity: There were outdoor and domestic electricity services, except in Carrizal on the Tambo river.

DESCRIPTION OF MODULE

Architecture: The improved 'quincha' housing module consisted of one room which was the initial stage of a home that could be gradually extended. The multi-purpose module has a built-up area of 24m^2 and a covered area of 28.8m^2.

Engineering: Conventional paving foundations with continuous footing. The structure (columns and beams) consists of sawn timber and logs (tornillo, eucalyptus); 'quincha' walls (ditch reed) plastered with mud and cement-sand, light roofing with Guayaquil cane rafters. Ditch reed roof covered with mud and plastered with cement-sand.

Finishing touches:
Polished cement flooring and pavement
Roof covering: pressed mud covered with cement-sand 1:5.
Outside walls: fully plastered
Columns and roof beam: varnished wood
Outdoor and indoor skirting: plaster
Lining of inside walls: fully plastered
General carpentry: iron on windows and doors.
Participation of the population
The population attended the training activities and contributed unskilled manpower.

DESIGN

The housing extension module consists of independent modules, taking the following into consideration:

The average area of the community plots, as well as the most common dimensions for the front and back of the plots.

The average slope of the land: in order to have rooms at different levels (construction of terraces, dry walls etc.).

The average number of family members.

The activities carried out in the home other than for domestic purposes (e.g. storeroom, crops, garage, animal-breeding); the latter is not advisable if the livestock involved are large animals like cattle).

Consequently, the design allowed for:

The distribution of rooms based on the above plan and on future water and sewage connections.

The location of social areas at the front, using the improved 'quincha' module for that purpose.

Indoor construction: the kitchen and the bathroom adjacent to facilitate water and sewage installation, thus saving on pipes and reducing humidity in the other rooms.

Building at the back of the property: bedrooms, storerooms and other rooms, depending on the number of people in each family, their occupations and the size of the land. In corner houses, the bedrooms were built next to the side property line alongside the other street, to complete the profile.

Access to the bedrooms, kitchen and bathroom is through a patio or roofed corridor, depending on the local climate and customs.

PREFABRICATED 'QUINCHA'

Negotiating and implementing agency: National Standardization, Training and Research Service for the Construction Industry – SENCICO (formerly ININVI).

Publication:
'Prefabricated quincha, manufacture and construction'. Reprint of the ININVI publication, 1997.

Investigation:
ININVI, unconventional construction system RM. N° 106-95-MTC/15.VC.

Housing: Various designs

Date: 1997 until 2002

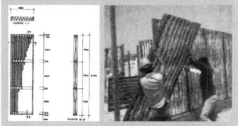

Typical 'quincha' panel

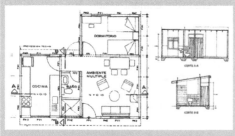

Typical housing model

Module under construction

Photographs: SENCICO publications.

PREFABRICATED 'QUINCHA' – ININVI-SENCICO

DESCRIPTION (*)

The prefabricated 'quincha' was made by filling wooden frames with pebbles, ditch reed or bamboo strips, braided to avoid using nails. Once the panels were mounted and fixed into the walls or the respective place, they were covered with mud mixed with straw to form a first layer. Then a final coat of plaster was applied, with mud, cement, plaster or other materials (depending on the climate, costs or preferences).

The light roofing was made of a wooden structure covered with cane and compacted mud with straw.

Climate considerations: in areas with heavy rainfall, asbestos-cement, zinc or other sheeting should be placed over the compacted mud.

BASIC MATERIALS

As a renewable resource, wood must be well dried and preserved. For resilience purposes, group C is required, with a 0.44 to 0.40 g/cm³ density, as it combines resilience, pliability and manufacturing techniques.

Cane: carrizo (Chusquea spp.), caña brava (Gynesium sagitarium), guadúa, bamboo and Guayaquil cane (Guadua angustifolia). 'Caña brava' or ditch reed, is preferable for 'quincha' panels because it lasts longer. Bamboo should be used for the roof.

THE PANEL

Comprised mainly of a structural frame made of sawn timber; a typical panel consists of two supports, four cross beams and four semi-diagonal beams.

The majority of the wooden pieces of the frame are 3 cm x 6.3 cm and 2 cm x 3.0 cm².

All the panels were 2.4m high, with two alternative widths: 0.6m and 12m.

The variety of panels was reduced as much as possible as this is a modular and rationalized prefabricated 'quincha' system.

DESCRIPTION OF THE MODULE

Architecture: The modular design of prefabricated 'quincha' panels should be considered. The length of all the rooms should be a multiple of 0.6m. The floor level should be at least +0.1m high, taking the front or surrounding pavement as a reference; the finished wall should be at least 0.1m thick.

A shed roof or gable roof are recommended, with an average slope of 15% to 30%. The descents should be long enough to prevent the walls from being dampened by the rain.

Engineering:

Conventional continuous foundation with a 1:12 cement-concrete mix. The footings were at least 0.2m. high, 1:8 cement-concrete mix and 1ft. stones.

Structure with sawn timber columns 6.5cm x 6.5cm section and 3.0m long; roof beams 6.5cm x 6.5cm and no more than 3.6m long.

Rectangular spaces were prepared for the sloping roof.

Bamboo cover to support the compacted mud and cement-sand plaster.

Finishing touches:
- Flooring and pavement: polished cement
- Covering: compacted mud plastered with cement-sand 1:5.
- Outside walls: fully plastered
- Columns and roof beam: varnished wood
- Indoor and outdoor skirting: plastered
- Covering of indoor walls: fully plastered
- General carpentry: wooden doors and windows

ADVANTAGES:

Due to its thermal qualities, 'quincha' adapted well to the local climate conditions. It is cool both during the day and at night; in addition, since local materials are used, the buildings are easily adaptable to local environmental characteristics.

There are plenty of materials available on the coast and in jungle fringe areas (alongside the rivers) and they grow quickly.

CONDITIONS AND LIMITATIONS

The cane should be mature and dry.

All the timber must be of a well-known long-lasting quality, and be treated against fungus and insects.

In damp areas such as the bathroom and kitchen, the wooden and cane surfaces must be covered with plaster or a waterproof overlay.

Skilled manpower and technical advice is required, which restricts community participation.

More technical assistance is required when an expansion involves building another floor.

CONCLUSIONS

The same procedure as for two-storey buildings, to which end an adequate structural design is required, bearing in mind the load between floors.

PARTICIPATION OF THE POPULATION

The population can be trained to fit the panels; however, skilled manpower is required to prepare them, as well as technical assistance for building the house.

EXPANSION

Independent one-storey modules are used to expand the dwellings. If the plans include adding another storey, the structural calculations of the columns must be made from the start.

(*) Taken from the prefabricated 'quincha' manual published by SENCICO.

REINFORCING ADOBE HOUSES

Research and implementing entity: Pontificate Catholic University of Peru (PUCP).

Financing: PUCP – CERESIS – GTZ.

Areas: Districts of Ancash, Cuzco, Tacna, Moquegua, Ica y La Libertad.

Number of houses: 19 pilot housing modules

Area of houses: 30,40m².

Cost of reinforcing the house: US$ 200.

Date: 1998

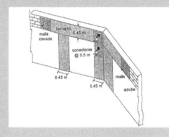

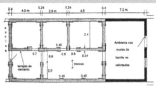

Reinforcement system: mesh and plate

ADVANTAGES
Quick, economical and efficient reinforcement of adobe brick houses in seismic areas.
Applicable to any type of adobe brick housing.
The system is easily understood and applicable by middle management technicians or the trained population.
The system can also be applied to new housing.

LIMITATIONS
This technique cannot be used to repair housing if the soil is of a poor quality and/or the density of the walls in the house is low.
It is used to prevent the house from collapsing; its application does not make a house earthquake-proof.

REINFORCED ADOBE HOUSES

OBJECTIVE (*)
A method to delay the collapse of 19 adobe houses, selected at random, so that the inhabitants have time to leave them in the event of an earthquake and thus save their lives. The PUCP investigated the quickest, most effective, economical and simple way to do so, employing electro-welded mesh with ¾ft holes and 1mm diameter.

LOCATION AND SURROUNDINGS
The project was implemented in six districts: Ancash, Tacna, Moquegua, Ica, La Libertad and Cuzco, at different altitudes above sea level and with different seismic characteristics. The selection criterion was that the walls and roofs of the houses should be slightly deteriorated.
The climate in these different areas varies from hot and dry to cold and dry. In most cases, the rainy season is from December to March, the volume ranging from minimal to regular. The characteristics of the land also vary.

District	Locality	Number of houses	Number of floors
Ancash	Pedregal Alto	1	1
	Centro Marian	1	1
	Olleros	1	1
	Huaraz	1	2
Tacna	Caplina	2	1
Maquegua	Yacango	1	1
	Estuquiña	2	1
Ica	Guadalupe	1	1
	Pachacutec	1	1
La Libertad	Las Delicias	2	1
	Simbal	1	1
	Barraza	1	1
Cuzco	Huasao	1	2
	Andahuaylillas	3	2

EXISTING INFRASTRUCTURE
Support for water, sewage and electricity services was not contemplated in the project.

DESCRIPTION OF THE MODULE
Architecture: The work was done on existing one or two-storey houses, the built-up area of which ranged from 24 m² to 34 m².
Engineering and reinforcement: mesh was fitted into the weaker areas. In the two-storey houses, horizontal strips of mesh were placed all around the ground floor, in addition to the vertical strips; in the second floor where the shear stress is weaker, horizontal and vertical strips of mesh were fitted in the top part of the walls.
Materials:
• Electro-welded mesh with ¾ft holes and 1mm diameter.
• Metal plates
• No. 8 interconnecting wire for the metal plates
• Mortar or plaster

PARTICIPATION OF THE POPULATION
The project provided technical advice and materials and local manpower was hired.

APPLICATION
Substantial defects were found in the houses, such as:
• Foundations slightly deteriorated by humidity.
• Walls as high as 5m, therefore it was necessary to put horizontal strips of mesh halfway across them.
• Fine cracks
• Adobes that disintegrated when drilled
• The spaces on gable roofs had to be reinforced with an additional horizontal bar. Defects that could not be restored were also found.
• Housing built on soil of a very poor quality
• Houses with no foundation
• Houses with more than two storeys and low density walls

REINFORCED ADOBE

Negotiating and implementing entity:
Disaster Prevention and Study Centre (PREDES)
Movement for Peace, Disarmament and Liberty (MPDL)
Financing:
European Commission Humanitarian Aid Office (ECHO).
Areas:
District municipalities of Puquina, Coalaque and Omate in the Sánchez Cerro province, district of Moquegua.
Number of houses:
250 housing modules.
Area of houses:
30.40 m² and 42.98m².
Cost of module:
US$ 1,121.48.
Date:
February and March 2002

Binding the Roof Beam

Finished housing module

ADVANTAGES

Making adobe houses more earth-quake-resilient using electro-welded mesh only increases their cost by approximately seventy dollars per module.

Due to its thermal qualities, adobe adapts well to the local climate conditions. It is cool both during the day and at night; in addition, since local materials are used, the buildings are easily adaptable to local environmental characteristics.

LIMITATIONS

In this case, it will be impossible to build a second floor.

- Walls badly eroded at their base
- Badly deteriorated or moth-eaten roofs
- Walls that were too long, more than 7m, without any centre bracing.
- Thresholds resting on loose adobe bricks.

(*)PUCP publication. Interview with Gladys Villagarcía, chief of the PUCP materials testing laboratory.

Reinforced Adobe – PREDES

LOCATION AND SURROUNDINGS (*)

The project was implemented in the Puquima, Coalaque and Omate districts located between 2,100 and 3,200m above sea level. There are seven settlements with a homogenous profile, with typical adobe buildings and galvanized zinc roofing.

The climate is mild in the lower areas (Challahuayo, Quinistacas, Coalaque, El Estanque), with an average annual temperature of 16°C, and cold in the higher areas (Puquina, Chacahuayo, Chuñuhuayo). The rainy season is from December to March and is generally moderate.

The land is fairly flat and regular, slightly undulating with small or medium slopes. The bearing capacity of the soil is 0.5 kg/cm². Target families own or have legal possession of the land where the housing modules were built.

EXISTING INFRASTRUCTURE

Water: there was a water supply system.
Sewage: in larger settlements, there was an outside sewage network; in smaller settlements, silos were used for excreta disposal purposes.
Electricity: there was an electricity service in all the settlements.

DESCRIPTION OF MODULE

Architecture: a two room, multiple purpose dwelling was designed, with a built-up area of 30.40 m² and a covered area of 42.98 m². A gradual future expansion was anticipated.
Engineering:
Foundation and footings: the foundation consisted of a 0.5m x 0.6m section with large angular stone masonry with cement-sand-lime mortar.
Structure: formed by 0.4 m thick octagonal, longitudinal and transversal adobe walls, reinforced with electro-welded mesh in all the corners indoors and outdoors, covered with cement-sand mortar. Reinforced concrete roof beam to confine the walls.
Roofing: gable roof with a 15% slope, rafters made of 2ft x 4ft tornillo wood, with 2ft x 3ft wooden cross-beams and 2ft x 2ft slats on top of them, onto which the 0.8m x 3.0m galvanized zinc sheeting was fitted.

Finishing touches:
- Flooring: polished cement
- Roof: galvanized zinc sheets painted with tile-coloured anticorrosive paint.
- Outside walls: fully plastered
- Roof beam: plastered on the outside
- Outside skirting: plastered
- Covering of inside walls: certain sections plastered with mesh.
- General carpentry: iron and glass on doors and windows

PARTICIPATION OF THE POPULATION

The project provided the materials, skilled manpower, training and technical advice for the construction of the initial rooms. Beneficiaries will build new rooms in their homes when they can afford to do so.

EXPANSION

The traditional use of adobe was taken into account and a flexible module was proposed so that the beneficiaries could expand their homes in the future.

(*) Taken from PREDES publications.
Photographs: PREDES.

ADOBE – PAR

Management and implementing entity:
Support Programme for the Repopulation and Development of Emergency Zones (PAR). Ministry of Women and Social Development

Financing:
Swiss Development Cooperation (SDC)

Location:
District municipality of Ayacucho.

House area:
On average: 60m².
Cost per module:
On average US$ 1500–3000
(= 5100–10200 soles)
Date: 2001 to 2002.

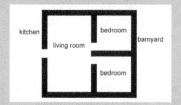

Housing diagram

Housing module and bathroom

Housing module and bathrooms

Advantages:
Adobe, due to its thermal qualities, adapts very well to the climate conditions of the location: it is cool during the day and maintains heat at night. Further, by making use of local materials, these constructions have appropriate environmental characteristics.

The materials are found in abundance in the area.

Constructed at double height so that the beneficiary could put in the mezzanine, allowing the construction to be led by an experienced technician, guaranteeing its quality.

Limitations:
Adobe requires lengthy work from the benefactors and requires a long time to dry.

ADOBE – PAR

FRAMEWORK AND OBJECTIVES
The project falls within the National Plan for Reconstruction after of political violence.

LOCATION AND SURROUNDINGS
The project was carried out in the district municipality of Ayacucho, in urban locations between 3000 and 3500 m above sea level.

The climate is cold and dry with predominately low temperatures. Rainfall is between December and March with a medium recorded volume.

The terrain is quite irregular, slightly undulating in the valleys and rugged towards the mountains.

Existing Infrastructure
Water: not connected to a drinking water supply system, water was procured from wells.

Drainage: small localities were not connected to a drainage network or to a sewage disposal system; instead they used septic tanks. Larger villages were connected to a sewage network.

Electricity: not connected to an electricity system.

MODULE DESCRIPTION
Architecture:
The housing module developed consisted of a multifunctional living space and two bedrooms. It was anticipated that they would be increased to two floors, as is the typical local model. The roof area was 60m².

A bathroom with a septic tanks was also constructed on each plot.

Engineering:
Conventional laying of floors, strip foundations and stem walls.

Structure: adobe brick walls 0.40m by 0.40m by 0.08m, plastered with mud and sand-cement; a light roof with eucalyptus joists or similar.

Wooden beam range, covered with sheets of corrugated iron and painted with an anti-corrosive coloured paint.

Finishing:
• Module floor and pathway: cement rendered.
• Module covering: mud bricks and coating of sand-cement 1:5.
• Coating of exterior walls: totally plastered.
• Wooden beams: varnished wood.
• Lower wall borders exterior and interior: plaster.
• Coating of interior walls: totally plastered.
• General carpentry: wood for the door and two windows.

10x10, QUINCHA, ADOBE AND CEMENT BLOCKS

Negotiating and implementing entity:
National Standardization, Training and Research Service for the Construction Industry – (SENCICO), CITED, UNI.

Financing:
CITED.

Place:
District municipality of Moquegua.

Number of houses:
10 experimental housing modules.

Area of the house:
37 m², 45 m², 50 m², 65 m².

Date: 2001 to 2002.

Quincha, adobe and cement block modules

ADVANTAGES

Quincha: Due to its earthquake-resilient qualities, it adapts well to local conditions.

Adobe: It has very good thermal and acoustic qualities. It is a traditional material in Moquegua.

Clement blocks:
Construction can take place on small plots and the building process is quick.

VILLAGE PARTICIPATION

A psychological resilience technique was used to develop abilities to positively confront adversity. Development groups were chosen from children and young people. Workshops were carried out focusing on this technique, which complements the construction of the housing. The project supplied the materials and technical advice for the construction of the initial module and trained participating families so that they worked as local labour force.

EXPANSION

The possibilities of housing growth were talked about with the beneficiary: if the beneficiary wanted to provide more material and additional labour, a double height module structure would be delivered. The basic module is one storey, made so that a wooden mezzanine could be added when the beneficiary had the resources. The additional contribution of PAR was the technical management of this expansion.

Material	Area (m²)	No. Houses	Cost Cost Soles/m²
Quincha	37–40	4	334
Adobe	50–65	3	311
Cement blocks	45	3	344

10x10, QUINCHA, ADOBE AND CEMENT BLOCKS – SENCICO

OBJECTIVE AND SCOPE

The objective of the project was to help the victims in Moquegua after the earthquake of 23rd June 2001.

The house covered functional needs, in keeping with the lifestyles of local citizens.

A financing requirement established by CITED was that the constructions were built with an experimental technology using various kinds of materials and building technologies.

Furthermore, a training workshop was organized for any of the victims willing to learn the construction systems.

LOCATION AND SURROUNDINGS

The project was implemented in Moquegua, located at 1,410 m.a.s.l. in a highly seismic area.

The climate is hot and dry, with predominantly high temperatures typical of a desert area. Strong winds blow in the afternoons. Rainfall is minimal, between December and March.

The land is fairly irregular, with moderate to steep slopes. The bearing capacity of the soil is very low and a soil survey was required. The quality of the soil in the city is very poor for earth constructions.

EXISTING INFRASTRUCTURE

Water: a water supply system was available.
Sewage: There was a sewage system available.
Electricity: Outdoor and domestic electricity services were available.

LIMITATIONS

Quincha: Due to its thermal qualities, it does not adapt well to the local climate, as it is fresh during the day but very cold at night.

Cane is susceptible to rotting when exposed.

The panels are difficult for the population to replicate, as they are made by a carpenter.

Adobe:

There is not much good quality earth available to prepare it. Due to the weight of the material, it requires a lot of effort and a long drying time; because of the earthquake-resilient characteristics, a lot of space is required on the plot.

DESCRIPTION OF MODULE

Architecture: The improved quincha module had one room, which comprised the initial stage of a 'quincha' house that would gradually be expanded. Each module consisted of a multi-purpose room with a built-up area of 24 m² and a covered area of 28.8 m².

Engineering: Conventional foundation with continuous footings (reinforced in some cases).

Structure: Prefabricated 'quincha' with standard sawn timber and ditch reed panels with a dome-shaped roof.

Adobe reinforced with cane, walls plastered with mud and cement-sand, light wooden roof with Technopor sheets. Finishing touches:

- Flooring and pavement: polished cement
- Covering: compacted mud or cement-sand plaster 1:5
- Covering of outside walls: fully plastered
- Columns and roof beam: varnished wood
- Indoor and outdoor skirting: plastered
- Covering of inside walls: fully plastered
- General carpentry: iron doors and windows.

PARTICIPATION OF THE POPULATION

The project worked on the housing design under an agreement with the National Engineering University (UNI). The work was completed by an architect and expert engineers.

The project provided the materials, skilled manpower and technical assistance for the housing construction, paying stipends to the beneficiaries of the homes and the beneficiaries of the training programme.

A special general primer was produced, containing criteria on the location, construction and finishing touches with each type of material.

Comments:

Projects of this type permit the dissemination of alternative technologies, however it is worth pointing out the following:

- The design made by the students was delivered late. Better results were obtained by working with a professional architect.
- A permanent construction instructor is required.
- The women responded very well in the workshops and as workers; however, men were better at specialized work such as the layout.
- The concrete block adapted better to the topographic characteristics of the region and better results were obtained.
- Prefabricated 'quincha' is difficult to replicate due to the specialization required for its initial preparation.
- Adobe is a costly foundation and requires a lot of space.
- The lesson obtained from experiments with various roofing alternatives was that they should be practical enough to be replicated without technical assistance.
- For the finishing touches and bathroom accessories, sponsorships and donations from companies like CELIMA were obtained.
- The cultivation of natural resources like cane, eucalyptus and other inputs used to prepare construction materials should be promoted.
  Interview with engineers Rafael Torres and Gabriela Esparza.
  Photographs: the authors

Annex 2 Analysis of the construction designs and experiences of PRACTICAL ACTION

The following pages contain a description of the projects undertaken by Practical Action (then called Intermediate Technology Development Group) in the Rioja and Moyobamba provinces situated in Alto Mayo in the district of San Martin: in Chuschi, Quispillacta and Uchuyri in the district of Ayacucho; in various neighbourhoods and in the Chen Chen plains in the city of Moquegua in the department of Moquegua; and in La Yarada in the district of Tacna.

As in the previous section, each project is presented in the form of summary records in which the aspects involved in each one of them can be easily appreciated. Included are a quantitative and qualitative summary of the projects, the length of each project, the location, the number of direct beneficiaries, the number of houses built, the type of module built and the technology employed, financial entities and their counterparts, the amount invested and some finer data such as the cost of each house in U.S. currency.

In addition, the specific objectives of each project are described, as well as background information, if any, the location and surroundings to indicate the climate and geography, existing infrastructure and the model and construction characteristics applied. Diagrams of the architectural and structural models of the houses are shown as well as photographs of the results obtained.

Aspects related to the participation of the community in each particular project are also mentioned.

Practical Action – ALTO MAYO

Negotiating and implementing entity:
Intermediate Technology Development Group – Practical Action Peru and Caritas del Peru.

Financing:
Caritas, Joint Fund Scheme, British Foreign Aid Office (ODA-JDS) and UNDP.

Counterpart organizations:
Caritas and beneficiary families.

Management:
Staff involved in the project: project manager, technical assistant, construction and promotion technicians, logistics and purchasing technicians. Temporary staff: a risk management technician, a geologist, Practical Action advisors.

Areas:
Soritor, Habana, Lliullucucha, Rioja, Moyobamba, Yantaló, Pasamano, Calzada, Jepelacio, Shucshuyacu, Marona, Posic, Tambo, El Porvenir, Yorongos, Palestina, La Libertad, Mashuyacu, Nuevo San Miguel, Las Palmeras, Santa Rosa de Tangumi, Tamboyacu in the department of San Martín.

Technology applied:
Improved quincha.

Direct benficiaries:
732 families from 16 towns in Alto Mayo.

Number of houses:
Phase 1 = 78 housing modules
Phase 2 = 480 housing modules.

Equipment:
24 classrooms and community buildings.

Area of houses:
28 m² and 30 m².

Total budget:
Phase 1 = US $ 120.000.

Cost of one module:
Phase 1 = US $ 1.538.
Phase 2 = US $ 600.

Date: 1991 to 1993.

SORITOR, HABANA, LLIULLUCUCHA, RIOJA, MOYOBAMBA, YANTALÓ, PASAMAYO, CALZADA, JEPELACIO, SHUCSHUYACU, MARONA, POSIC, TAMBO, EL PORVENIR, YORONGOS, PALESTINA, LA LIBERTAD, MASHUYACU, NUEVO SAN MIGUEL, LAS PALMERAS, SANTA ROSA DE TANGUMI, TAMBOYACU

INITIATION AND OBJECTIVES

Practical Action had been conducting a study on the socio-economic circumstances in the area when the earthquake occurred on 20th May 1990. Caritas called upon Practical Action to begin the Alto Mayo Reconstruction Project to help the victims in Soritor. Practical Action directors and experts drew up a proposal, placing emphasis on the use of local resources, the popular management of technologies and the protagonist role of the victims themselves. Discussions began from one neighbourhood to another, during which compacted mud and adobe constructions were discarded as being inappropriate for the local seismic conditions. The initial pilot project helped build demonstration classrooms and community centres made of improved quincha.

Context of intervention

Rural context

Townscape

LOCATION AND SURROUNDINGS

The project was implemented in the upper reaches of the Mayo river, in the Moyabamba and Rioja provinces of the district of San Martin, located between 450 and 700m above sea level and between 100 and 250m above sea level.

The climate is hot and damp, with predominantly high temperatures typical of a tropical area. The rainy season is from December to March, although there is very little rain.

The land is fairly irregular; the bearing capacity of the soil is 0.5 kg/cm².

EXISTING INFRASTRUCTURE

Architecture:
The improved 'quincha' housing module consisted of three rooms: a dining room-kitchen, a bedroom and a bathroom. The module was the initial stage of a 'quincha' house that could later be expanded on the second floor, to which end a staircase was anticipated. Each module had a built-up area of 25 cm² and a covered area of approximately 28.8 m².

Engineering: improved 'quincha'
Conventional foundation with floor plates and continuous footing.

Structure (columns and beams) of sawn timber and logs (tornillo, eucalyptus); 'quincha' walls (ditch reed) plastered with mud and cement-sand, light roofing with wooden rafters, covered with fibrocement tiles.

Finishing touches:
• Flooring and pavement: polished cement
• Covering: compacted mud plastered with cement-sand 1:5
• Covering of outside walls: fully plastered
• Columns and roof beam: varnished wood
• Inside and outside skirting: plaster
• Covering of inside walls: fully plastered
• General carpentry: Iron in doors and windows

MANAGEMENT

Practical Action and Caritas: project manager, construction instructor, technical assistant, construction and promotion technicians, logistics and purchasing technicians. Temporary staff: an external evaluator, a risk management trainer, a geologist, Practical Action advisors.

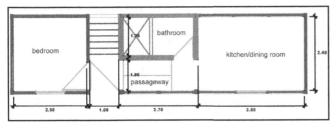

Improved 'quincha' module: plan view

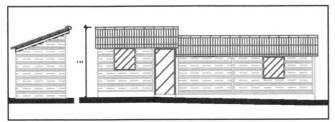

Improved 'quincha' module: side and front elevations

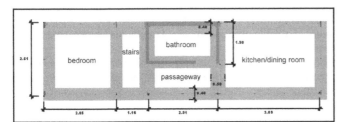

Improved 'quincha' module: foundation

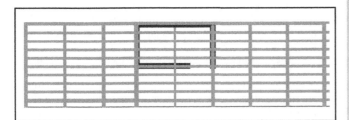

Improved 'quincha' module: rafters

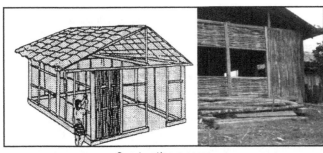

Construction process

Traditional house

Traditional house

Improved quincha module

Construction process

Finished house

Practical Action – ALTO MAYO

Project management
Intermediate Technology Development Group – Practical Action Peru, Caritas del Peru, Swiss Cooperation – COSUDE.

Financing:
Cáritas del Perú.

Areas:
Soritor, Habana, Lliullucucha, Rioja, Moyobamba, Yantaló, Pasamayo Calzada, Jepelacio, Shucshuyacu Marona, Posic, Tambo, El Porvenir, Yorongos, Palestina, La Libertad, Mashuyacu, Nuevo San Miguel, Las Palmeras, Santa Rosa de Tangumi and Tamboyacu in the department of San Martín.

Technology applied:
Improved 'quincha'.

INTERVENTION

Advantages:
- Excellent seismic resilience
- Construction inputs such as timber and substitutes fairly similar to cane are available locally.
- Building with 'quincha' was already a tradition introduced by migrants from Cajamarca.

Limitations:
- Although the use of recycled materials from destroyed houses speeds up the reconstruction process, in the end the houses may not last as long.
- Improved 'quincha' houses last longer if they are well maintained (every ten years), bearing in mind the preservation of the wood and cane components with adequate products.

SORITOR, HABANA, LLIULLUCUCHA, RIOJA, MOYOBAMBA, YANTALÓ, PASAMAYO, CALZADA, JEPELACIO, SHUCSHUYACU, MARONA, POSIC, TAMBO, EL PORVENIR, YORONGOS, PALESTINA, LA LIBERTAD, MASHUYACU, NUEVO SAN MIGUEL, LAS PALMERAS, SANTA ROSA DE TANGUMI, TAMBOYACU

CONTRIBUTIONS OF PRACTICAL ACTION AND THE POPULATION
The families were loaned galvanized zinc sheets, nails, wire and cement and they also received technical advice. They contributed timber, concrete, cane and family manpower.

Reconstruction stages:
1. The reconstruction began immediately after the earthquake, with financing from Caritas del Peru and the assistance of the municipality. Practical Action contributed the technological aspects and other institutions provided machinery, equipment and materials. The population was also eager to participate in the reconstruction work.
   During this first stage involving the construction of 'quincha' housing, material from destroyed homes was used, such as beams and wooden columns, among others. These recycled items and the help provided by organizations lowered the costs, therefore more houses were built. Galvanized zinc sheeting was used for the roofs. The housing modules built with the participation of the population were part of an experimental pilot project.
2. Two years after the earthquake, the housing construction process continued; however, by then the local contribution of recycled materials had been depleted and aid institutions had withdrawn their aid, therefore completely new materials of a better quality were used to build the houses, particularly sawn timber. Although the construction process slowed down, the experience acquired in previous constructions and the new material employed, improved the quality considerably. In this new stage, assistance was obtained from the Swiss Cooperation agency – COSUDE, which held a workshop on roof tiles with the technical supervision of a well-known company. The tiles were well made and the fact that they could easily be replaced when broken was an advantage. The workshop was very successful and well attended by the population.
3. When Practical Action and COSUDE withdrew from this area, Caritas was left in charge of the housing reconstruction process, but with a lower budget that limited the supply of materials for the beneficiaries. Consequently, they were supposed to plaster the outside walls of their homes on their own. The population organised a workshop with local people who had participated in the COSUDE workshops and who created their own type of tiles which they called 'Qataycreto', which were smaller and could only be used for future constructions.

Thirteen years since the reconstruction, all the 'quincha' houses in poor urban fringe and rural areas are still standing, but nearly 30% of the 'quincha' homes built in town centres have been replaced by concrete houses. This is due to the installation of a cement factory in Rioja, which carried out an aggressive campaign promoting the use of this material, as well as the soft loans granted by the Development Compensation Fund – FONCODES and the Materials Bank – BENMAT.

COMMENTS
The validity of the reconstruction is upheld by the large number of houses built at a low cost, which was made possible thanks to the materials recycled from destroyed houses.
In order to reduce the deterioration of the buildings, the recycled materials were carefully selected and those that were 60% deteriorated were cast aside. Furthermore, the unions between the wooden columns and the foundation were made waterproof to prevent the columns from rotting.
'Quincha' houing should be maintained at least every ten years, replacing deteriorated materials. In addition, for future maintenance purposes, roof tiles or other construction components should be provided as spares or as samples to be reproduced by the beneficiaries.
Plans processed by the authors.
Diagrams and photographs: Practical Action.

Practical Action – ALTO MAYO

Negotiating and implementing entity:
Intermediate Technology Development Group – Practical Action Peru, Caritas del Peru, Swiss Cooperation – COSUDE.

Financing:
Cáritas del Perú.

Areas:
Soritor, Habana, Lliullucucha, Rioja, Moyobamba, Yantaló, Pasamayo Calzada, Jepelacio, Shucshuyacu Marona, Posic, Tambo, El Porvenir, Yorongos, Palestina, La Libertad, Mashuyacu, Nuevo San Miguel, Las Palmeras, Santa Rosa de Tangumi y Tamboyacu; en el departamento de San Martín.

Technology applied:
Improved 'quincha'.

INTERVENTION

Advantages:
- Excellent resistance to earthquakes.
- Construction materials can be found in the area, for example wood substitutes such as sugar cane.

Limitations:
- Although the use of recycled materials from destroyed housing speeds reconstruction activities, in the long term the new homes may not be as durable.
- The lifetime of houses with 'quincha' can be prolonged to ten years with good maintenance, but you have to have the appropriate wood and cane products for preservation.

AYACUCHO: CHUSCHI, QUISPILLACTA and UCHUYRI

OBJECTIVES
The objective of the intervention in these towns affected by the earthquake of 31st October 1999 was to transfer the appropriate technology and the knowledge of risk management and disaster reduction procedures, based on the reconstruction process. The population of Ayacucho is one of the poorest in the country. The GDP per capita is one of the lowest of all the departments in Peru.

Consequently, the project's intention was to provide construction training to the target population so that they would acquire working skills. Local people were also given practical training on housing construction and the installation of sanitation systems, employing appropriate technologies for the area, based on the utilization of local resources and materials.

LOCATION AND SURROUNDINGS
The Chuschi area consists of five neighbourhoods comprised of the peasant communities of Quispillacta and Uchuyri in the Cangallo province, district of Ayacucho, 118km south of the capital city of that district. It is located at an altitude of 3,141m above sea level.

EXISTING INFRASTRUCTURE
Water: There were no safe water supply networks in this area. Sewage: there were no sewage services in this area.
Electricity: There were electricity grids in the area.

DESCRIPTION OF PROJECT
The project achieved its goal to build a total of 213 houses, 100 bathrooms and 6 community buildings to be used as a school, church, medical post and meeting centres. It also repaired 25 roofs.

TARGET POPULATION
Direct beneficiaries were 338 families or approximately 1,690 people. Indirect beneficiaries were the three communities that can make use of the community buildings.

MANAGEMENT
Project staff: project manager, three construction and promotion technicians, a social communicator, a civil engineer, an accountant and a geographer.
Temporary staff: an anthropologist, a risk management trainer, interviewers and surveyors and Practical Action consultants.

District-Province	Locality	Technology	Number of Homes
Ayacucho, Cangallo	Chuschi	Adobe	74
	Quispillacta	Adobe	118
	Uchuyri	Adobe	21
		Total	213

Maps, photographs and diagrams: the authors.

Practical Action – AYACUCHO CHUSCHI, QUISPILLACTA and UCHUYRI

The better standard of living and family and community integration improved the access to housing and community buildings.

Community building: Church

Community building

Finished module

Expansions and improvements

The bathroom improved people's health and lifestyles

AYACUCHO: CHUSCHI, QUISPILLACTA and UCHUYRI

ARCHITECTURE

The housing module derived from previous research carried out in the Ayacucho project and from the optimization of the adobe technology. It had between one and three rooms, depending on the topography it was adapted to. They were all one storey homes with a built-up area ranging from 24m² to 42m².

ENGINEERING, REINFORCEMENT

The adobe brick walls were reinforced with cane horizontally and cross-wise, with a tie beam at the top of the walls, a sawn timber roof and wooden brace beams, covered with cement tiles referred to as 'Qataycreto'. No vertical construction was anticipated.
The bathrooms were also built of adobe and contained sanitary fixtures and a septic tank.

Materials:
• Farm soil.
• Sawn timber and eucalyptus logs.
• Qataycreto tiles.
• Wooden doors and windows
• Ceramic floor
• Cement toilet

PARTICIPATION OF THE POPULATION

The project provided technical assistance, materials, training for the beneficiaries and technical advice for the construction.
The campaign to implement the project was supported by municipal authorities, community authorities, civil organisations and local ecclesiastic organisations.
The population carried out the work under the traditional system of mutual aid referred to as 'aini'; they also provided some materials.
Risk management workshops were held for the people in each area.
The beneficiaries themselves evaluated their participation.
Selection of beneficiaries: the selection criteria took into consideration the affected families, single mothers or widows, victims suggested by local authorities and leaders, whose properties were legally unencumbered.

PROCEDURES

Programming the activities and establishing rules for the participation. A certificate and the housing plan were handed to each of the beneficiaries upon the completion of the works.
A regular flow of communication took place during the implementation of the project.
The victims elected their representatives to deal with the authorities and Practical Action.
In Quispillacta, advantage was taken of the presence of the varayoc as the community authority.

TRAINING

The objective was to create risk management skills and strengthen the population's capacity to recover themselves, their traditions and their construction techniques. All social agents were involved in the workshops, to achieve community development and long-term replication.
The time devoted to the training allowed the beneficiaries to understand and commit themselves to the project. The participation of a bilingual social communicator was necessary, as the sessions were held entirely in Quechua.
At each stage of the project, training was provided in accordance with the component of the construction process. In the workshops, the people were taught to make adobe, to draw up 1:1 scale models, to apply the adobe reinforced with cane construction technique and the roofing technique and to understand the need to protect the houses from dampness and erosion. This technique was essential for transmitting know-how in an educational and illustrative manner. Finally, replicas were made of adobe bricks, clay floors, roof tiles and models of doors and windows.
Plans processed by the authors. Photographs: the authors.

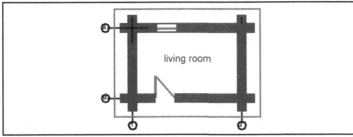

'R1 adobe module: plant' ?

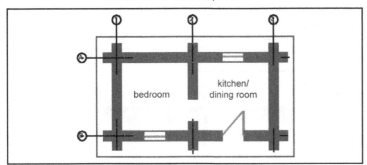

R2 adobe module: plan

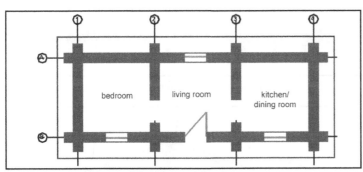

R3 adobe module: plan

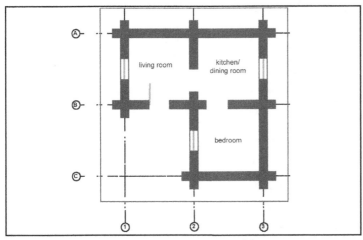

L-shaped adobe module: plant

Practical Action-AYACUCHO CHUSCHI, QUISPILLACTA and UCHUYRI REINFORCED ADOBE MODULES:

Three types of modules of the following dimensions:

R1 = 23,32 m².
R2 = 28,96 m².
R3 = 42,20 m².
L = 42,20 m².

The area of the bathrooms is 2,89 m².
The area of community buildings is 45,36 m².

ModuleR1

Module R2

Module R3

L-shaped module

Adobe module elevations

Practical Action – AYACUCHO

CHUSCHI, QUISPILLACTA and UCHUYRI ADOBE REINFORCED WITH CANE ENGINEERING

Foundations: 70% large stones, max. 12' + 30% simple concrete 1:10.

Footing: 75% medium stones, max. 6' + 25% simple concrete 1:8. Walls made of bricks that had no more than 0,2% to 30% of salts; no more than 18% clay and between 50% and 75% sand. Sifting with N° 4 mesh. Finishing with cement plaster. Roof, 50 kg/cm^2 overload. Wooden doors and windows

Beam union

Details of beams, crossbars and wall

Roofing with Qataycreto

Adobe walls

Expansions and improvements

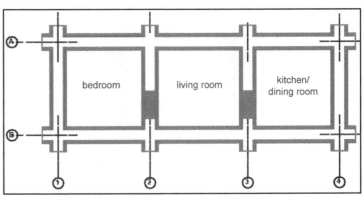

Typical foundation: plan view

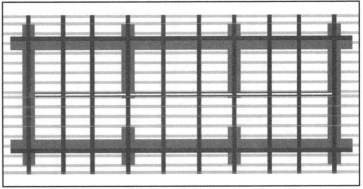

Structure of a typical roof

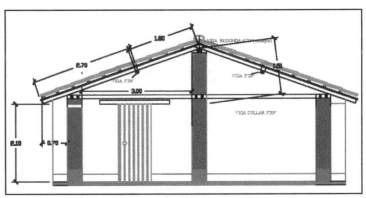

Adobe structure: Typical shear of R2

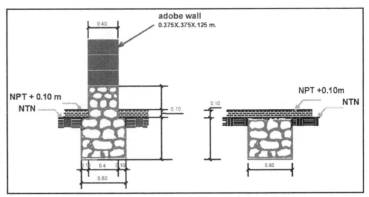

Typical foundation details

Practical Action – MOQUEGUA

Researching and implementing entities:
Intermediate Technology Development Group – Practical Action Peru, Development Education and Promotion Centre (CEOP-ILO).

Financing:
German Agro Action – German Ministry for Economic Co-operation and Development (BMZ), Sustained Development Foundation (FUNDESO).

Area:
Department of Moquegua; Mariscal Nieto province; Los Ángeles, San Antonio, San Francisco, Mariscal Nieto and Pampas de Chen Chén.

Population beneficiaries:
195 families = 975 people

Number of houses:
Moquegua: 195 housing modules

Technology applied:
Adobe: Moquegua I and Moquegua II.
Cement blocks: Moquegua III.

Area of house:
34 m² to 48 m².

Cost per house:
US$ 2.224

Date:
August 2001 to April 2003.

ADOBE REINFORCED WITH CANE

ADVANTAGES
- An easy to understand and apply system for mid-level technicians or trained people.
- Improved technology applied to traditional construction.

LIMITATIONS
- Poor quality soil.
- Construction is slow due to the preparation process of the adobe bricks.
- Little space to dry and then build with adobe.
- The construction of a large number of houses damages the quality of the productive soil.
- For women, older people or disabled people, the production of adobe requires great effort due to the weight of the material.

MOQUEGUA I: LOS ANGELES, SAN FRANCISCO, SAN ANTONIO AND MARISCAL NIETO MOQUEGUA II: MARISCAL NIETO AND MACCHU PICHU MOQUEGUA III: PAMPAS DE CHEN CHÉN

OBJECTIVE
Build homes for extremely poor families affected by the earthquake and develop skills for the application of improved adobe construction technologies.
The first stage of the project was implemented by the Practical Action – CEOP-ILO consortium.

View of the city of Moquegua

LOCATION AND SURROUNDINGS
Moquegua, the capital city of the department of Moquegua situated at 1,400m above sea level. was affected by the earthquake of 23rd June 2001 (6.9 degrees on the Richter scale). The main factors that caused the high level of damages were the poor quality of the soil and the location of the houses on unstable slopes.
The city is located in an area comprised of four different zones: (i) the low zone comprised of alluvial terraces formed by the Tumilaca river and its affluents; (ii) the intermediate zone on a slightly undulating surface, leaning towards the valley, formed by the colluvial deposits superimposed on alluvial deposits and clayey strata; (iii) the central zone situated on sedimentary soil; and (iv) the high zone which has a mixed relief, with steep slopes modified by the occupation process. The city develops in the central zone with an octagonal layout that was originally 4m to 5m per section and constructions at a pavement level. Traditional buildings are adobe brick on the first floor and 'quincha' on the second-storey.
The climate varies depending on the season, from hot and dry to cold and dry. Minimal rainfall between December and March.

THE PROJECT
The project consisted of three stages referred to as Moquegua I, Moquegua II and Moquegua III, implemented between August 2001 and April 2003. The construction technology applied was adobe in Moquegua I and Moquegua II and concrete blocks in Moquegua III.

District and province	Location	Technology	No. of houses	Stage
Moquegua, Mariscal Nieto	Los Angelas	Adobe	103	Moquegua I
	Mariscal Nieto	Adobe	42	Moquegua II
	Chen Chén	Cement blocks	50	Moquegua III

Plans, maps and photographs processed by the authors.

Practical Action – MOQUEGUA

Traditional saddle roof

Module R2

Module R3

L-shaped module

View of the complex

MOQUEGUA I and MOQUEGUA II

ARCHITECTURE
The housing module was similar to the one applied in the Chuschi project, with two to three rooms adapted to the topography of the area. All the houses were single-storey homes. A formal contribution was the recovery of the traditional architecture of Moquegua, the 'saddle' or gable roof. The built-up areas varied between 34 m² and 48 m². They all had sanitary and electrical fixtures. A septic tank was included.

ENGINEERING, REINFORCED ADOBE
Adobe was used in the Moquegua I and II stages, this being the most accessible material traditionally used in the area due to its thermal qualities. The project considered adobe walls reinforced with frames, incorporating the wall structure. Difficulties were encountered with the construction systems initially proposed due to the limited local inputs. Temporary workshops were held to manufacture prefabricated vibrated concrete elements.

Materials:
- Farm soil
- Sawn timber for the beams and frames, prepared by local artisans
- Qataycreto tiles
- Cement
- Gravel, coarse sand
- Construction iron and wire
- Wooden doors and windows made by local carpenters.
- Porcelain sanitary fixtures

MANAGEMENT
In the implementation of Moquegua I, CEOP ILO helped select the beneficiaries, supervise the construction and provide skilled staff. The Moquegua II and II stages were implemented by Practical Action.
Project staff: project manager, four construction and promotion technicians, a nurse, a psychologist, two civil engineers, an accounting assistant and a logistics and construction technician.
Temporary staff: a risk management trainer, a geologist, interviewers and surveyors and consultants provided by CEOP ILO and Practical Action.

PARTICIPATION OF THE POPULATION
The project provided the materials, training for beneficiaries and technical advice for the construction. The implementation actions were partially supported by municipal authorities, community authorities, civil organizations and ecclesiastic organizations like Caritas.
The beneficiaries contributed materials and manpower.

PROCEDURES
The selection criteria took into account the poorest affected families with children, single mothers or widows, the disabled, the victims suggested by local authorities and leaders, whose properties were legally unencumbered.
The beneficiaries themselves evaluated their participation.
The acceptance certificate and the plan of the house was handed to each beneficiary upon the completion of the construction work.

COMMUNICATION
During the implementation of the project, a regular flow of communication was maintained between the staff involved and the beneficiaries, which began when the materials were handed over at the initial meetings and continued throughout the construction and training process.

TRAINING
In the workshops, the people were taught how to prepare adobe, 1:1 scale models were drawn up, construction techniques were applied with adobe reinforced with cane, the roofing technique was taught as well as the requirements for protecting the houses against humidity and erosion. This technique was essential for transmitting knowledge in an educational and illustrative manner. In the end, the trainees were able to replicate the fitting of adobes, clay floors, roof tiles and doors and windows.
Photographs: Practical Action.

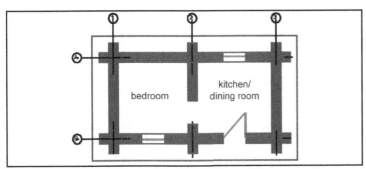

Module R2 of adobe: floor plan

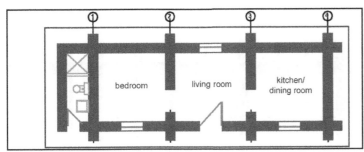

Module R3 of adobe: floor plan

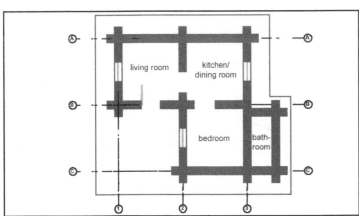

L-shaped module of adobe: floor plan

Finished adobe modules

Practical Action – MOQUEGUA MOQUEGUA I – MOQUEGUA II

ARCHITECTURE
Three types of modules:
R2 = 28,96 m².
R3 = 42,20 m². L = 42,20 m².
Bathrooms = 3.00 m².

ENGINEERING: REINFORCED ADOBE
Foundations: 70% large stones, max. 12″ + 30% simple concrete 1:10.
Footing: 75% medium stones, max. 6″ + 25% simple concrete 1:8. Walls made with adobes containing no more than 0.2% to 30% salts, no more than 18% clay and 50% to 75% sand, sifted with No. 4 mesh.
Walls finished with cement plaster. Roofing, 50 kg/cm² overload
Wooden doors and windows.

Module R2

Module R3

Indoor details and outdoor details (beneficiary's contribution)
Construction details

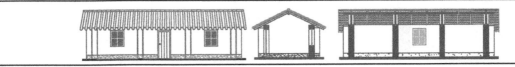

Adobe module: elevation and typical shears

Practical Action – MOQUEGUA MOQUEGUA I – MOQUEGUA II

ENGINEERING – ADOBE REINFORCED WITH CANE

Foundation: 70 % large stones, max. 12" + 30% simple concrete 1:10.

Footing: 75% medium stones, max. 6' +25% simple concrete 1:8. Walls made with adobes containing no more than 0,2% to 30% salts; no more than 18% clay and between 50% and 75% sand, sifted with No. 4 mesh. Finishing with cement plaster. Roofing, 50 kg/cm² overload.

Wooden doors and windows

Detail of frames and wall

Construction system

Reinforced walls and window

Overall view

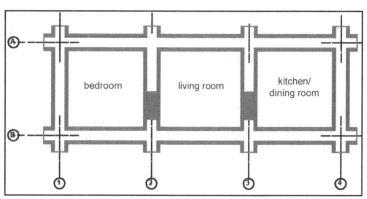

Typical foundation: floor plan

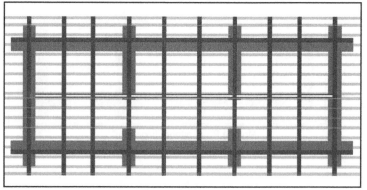

Structure of the typical roof

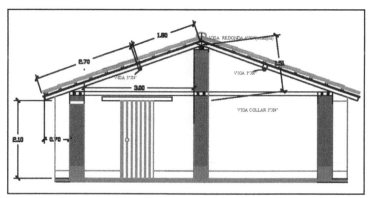

Adobe structure: typical shear

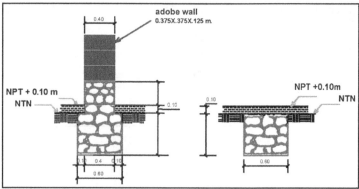

Typical foundation details

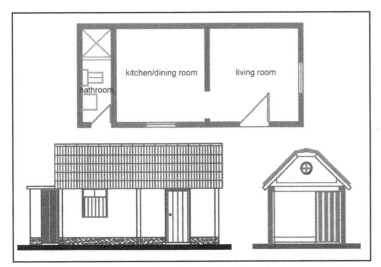

Module R2 in cement blocks: floor plan

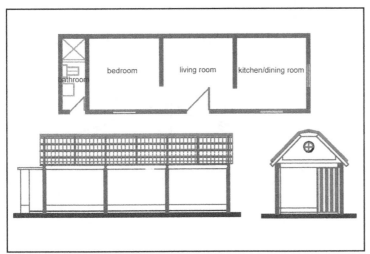

Module R3 in cement blocks: floor plan

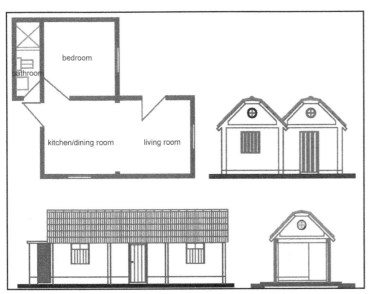

Modules in cement blocks: floor plan and elevations

Practical Action – MOQUEGUA
MOQUEGUA III
PAMPAS DE CHEN CHÉN

CEMENT BLOCK MODULE:
ARCHITECTURE:

The housing comes in the following types:

R2 = 28.96m² plus a bathroom of 3.00 m²

R3 = 42.20m² plus a bathroom of 3.00m²

ELE = 42.20m² plus a bathroom of 3.00 m²

Module R2

Module R2

Module R3

Module R3

L-shaped module

End of construction work.

Practical Action – MOQUEGUA
MOQUEGUA III
CEMENT BLOCK MODULES
ENGINEERING:
Foundations: 70% large stones, max. 12″ + 30% simple concrete 1:8. Footing: 75% medium stones, max. 6″ +25% simple concrete 1:7. Walls made with vibrated concrete blocks with cavities that must not exceed 25% of their volume, resilient to 25 kg/cm² compression. Covering of beams and columns 2.5cm. Wooden doors and windows

Module R2

Details of the beams, cross bars, quincha tympanum, adobe wall and Qataycreto cover

'Tumbadillo' Glued and painted cloth ceiling

Construction detail and bathroom

Contribution to the design of an L-shaped module

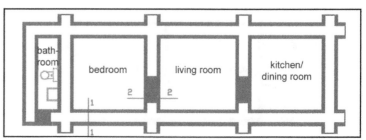

Typical foundation: floor plan

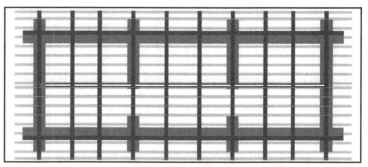

Structure of the typical roof

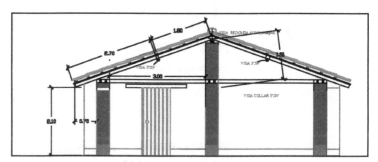

Adobe structure: typical shear

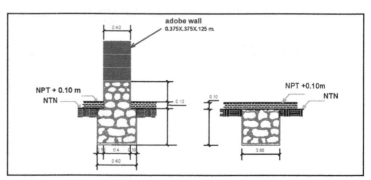

Typical foundation details: shears

Overall view

LA YARADA: LAS PALMERAS and LOS OLIVOS

Practical Action – TACNA

Investigating and implementing entity: Intermediate Technology Development Group – Practical Action Peru.

Financing: Sustained Development Foundation (FUNDESO) and Generalitat de Catalunya, Italian Mission, Callosa de Segura Parrish-Alicante.

Supervision:
United Nations Development Programme (UNDP).

Management: Project staff: Project manager, three construction and promotion technicians, an accounting assistant. **Temporary staff:** a risk management trainer, a geographer, interviewers and surveyors, Practical Action consultants.

Las Palmeras and Los Olivos, La Yarada, department of Tacna.

Beneficiaries:
64 families = 320 people.

Nunber of houses:
64 houses.

Technology applied:
Cement blocks.

Area of house:
25.40 m² to 35.50 m².

Cost per house:
US $ 1.449 a US $ 2.040

Total cost of project:
US $ 98.000

Date:
February to December 2002.

CONCRETE BLOCKS

ADVANTAGES
- The system is easy for middle management technicians or the trained population to understand and apply. Not much supervision by experts is required.
- The quick building time: 13 cement blocks per square metre of wall.
- The reinforced masonry structure is easy to assemble.
- They are fire resistant
- The blocks are very appropriate for the characteristics of the seaside surroundings.

LIMITATIONS
- The building costs more because the foundation must be reinforced due to the low resilience of the sandy soil.
- There is not enough good quality water in the area.

OBJECTIVES

Rebuild the homes of the victims of the 23rd June 2001 earthquake, using cement blocks and an appropriate technology for the area and provide construction training to the target population in order to create work skills.

LOCATIONS m²

m² by the earthquake in the department of Tacna were concentrated in the districts located to the north of the city of Tacna, mostly the constructions built during the last 30 years on poor quality soil on the outskirts of the city. The worst off were the rural houses located in Pampa La Yarada – situated 45km from the city of Tacna at 10m above sea level on the coast, on very sandy soil.

With a homogeneous geomorphology, La Yarada is situated on a plain with soil that is inappropriate for foundations, with a bearing capacity of 0.5 to 1.5 kg/cm². In stratigraphic terms, the first layer is comprised of fill, sand and clay with a high content of salts and carbonates on top of quaternary deposits produced by floods and mudflows. That is why the majority of these houses collapsed.

The climate varies depending on the season, from hot-dry to cold-damp, with minimal rainfall between December and March. Strong winds are a characteristic of this area.

The project intervened in two areas: Las Palmeras and Los Olivos. Los Olivos is a town located 4 km from the coastal strip at 10m above sea level. The level of underground water is between 50m and 80m deep. Las Palmeras is situated a few minutes away from Los Olivos, less than 1km away from the coastal strip and at 10m above sea level. The water table is between 5m and 12m. deep.

Most of the people in the La Yarada area are migrants from the department of Puno, particularly from the Ilave province, who maintain the strong cultural traditions of their native area. They communicate in Aymara and preserve the 'aini' community work tradition. They also have very strong ties with their relatives, which was ideal for group work.

View of Pampa La Yarada

EXISTING INFRASTRUCTURE

Water: there were no water supply networks in either of the two places.
Sewage: there were no sewage or excreta disposal services in either of these areas.
Electricity: there were electricity grids in both places.

The single stage referred to as La Yarada was implemented between July and December 2002, with vibrated concrete blocks. This took place at the same time as the activities of the Moquegua II project.

The following was taken into consideration in the project: Due to the fragmented ownership of land and the organisation of productive activities around wells from which all the irrigation water is obtained, these were used as a source of water for construction purposes. Each well supplies water to an average of 15 families.

The houses that collapsed had been built with adobe and/or concrete blocks with no technical criteria, with reed mats or galvanized zinc sheeting for the roof.

District and province	Locality	No. of homes	Community centre
Tacra	La Yarada – Las Palmeras	37	01
Tacra	La Yarada – Los Olivos	27	–

Plans and maps processed by the authors. Photographs: the authors and Practical Action.

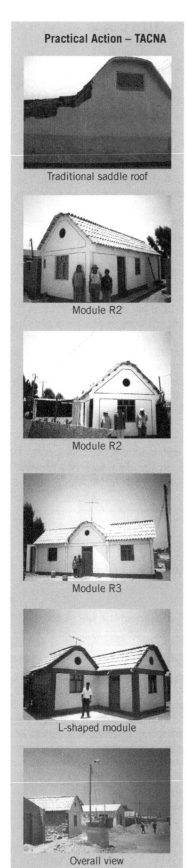

Practical Action – TACNA

Traditional saddle roof

Module R2

Module R2

Module R3

L-shaped module

Overall view

LA YARADA: LAS PALMERAS AND LOS OLIVOS

ARCHITECTURE
The housing module is similar to the one applied in the Moquegua project, with two or three rooms (no major difficulties were encountered due to the flat topography). All the houses were single storey homes. The 'saddle' or gable roof was used, as this is similar to the traditional Tacna architecture. The built-up areas varied between 25.4m² and 35.5m². All the modules had sanitary and electrical fixtures as well as a septic tank. The walls indoors and outdoors were plastered with cement and sand and the floors were polished cement.

ENGINEERING, REINFORCEMENT
In La Yarada, vibrated concrete blocks were used, this being the most appropriate system, given the manufacturing potential in the area and the climate conditions. The earthquake resilience of the constructions was good and thermal comforts were achieved with the architectural design. The use of cement blocks is common in Tacna and the materials for making them are available locally. The greatest problem was the high content of salt in the water.
A prefabricated reinforced concrete saddle roof was incorporated and flat roof tiles were applied, which proved to be more effective for preventing dust from entering the house. Temporary workshops were held to manufacture the prefabricated vibrated concrete elements.

Materials:
- Cement.
- Gravel, coarse sand.
- Construction iron and wire.
- Wooden doors and windows made by local carpenters.
- Porcelain sanitary fixtures.

PARTICIPATION OF THE POPULATION
The project provided the materials, training for the beneficiaries and technical advice for the construction.
For implementation purposes, the project relied on the organization experience of the people's native communities, based on the principle of reciprocity.
The beneficiaries provided manpower and/or materials.
The beneficiaries themselves evaluated their participation.

PROCEDURES
Selection criteria: the affected families had to be residents of the area, single mothers or widows and victims suggested by local authorities and leaders, whose properties were legally unencumbered. Another requirement was that they must not own another house.
The selection was made by Practical Action. Activities were programmed and rules for the participation were established.
The participation commitment expected by the project was established.
An acceptance certificate and a plan of the house were handed to each beneficiary upon the completion of the construction work.

COMMUNICATION
During the implementation of the project, a regular flow of conversation was maintained between the staff involved and the beneficiaries, which began at the meetings at which the materials were delivered and continued throughout the construction work and during the training process.

TRAINING
Risk management workshops were held in each place.
A temporary workshop was held to produce cement blocks, saddle roofs, micro-concrete roof tiles and covers for septic tanks, as well as preparing the steel for the beams and columns that would be used in the houses. At these workshops, photographs, videos, plans and scale models were shown, as well as a display of construction elements, cement block preparation and construction techniques, the roofing technique and the requirements to protect the houses from dampness and erosion.

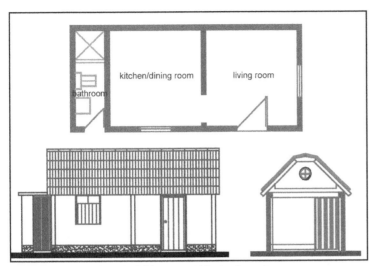

Module R2 in cement blocks: floor plan

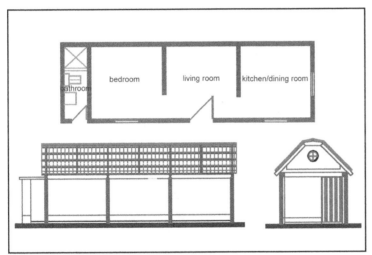

Module R3 in cement blocks: floor plan

Cement block modules: floor plan and elevations

Practical Action – TACNA
LA YARADA
PAMPAS DE CHEN CHÉN

CEMENT BLOCK MODULE ARCHITECTURE:
Three types of modules:
R2 = 28.96 m² plus a 3,00 m² bathroom.
R3 = 42.20 m² plus a 3,00 m² bathroom.
L = 42.20 m² plus a 3,00 m² bathroom.

Module R2

Module R3 construction system

L-shaped module

L-shaped module

Completed work

Practical Action – TACNA
LA YARADA

CONCRETE BLOCK
ENGINEERING Foundation:
70% large stones, max. 12"+30% simple concrete 1:8. Footing: 75% medium stones, max. 6"+25% simple concrete 1:7. Walls made with vibrated concrete blocks with cavities that do not exceed 25% of their volume, 25 kg/cm² resilience to compression.

2.5 cm. Covering on beams and columns. Wooden doors and Windows.

Detail of the wall and beam union

Detail of cement blocks, beams, tympanum and covering

Details of the saddle roof and covering

Preparing the saddle roof

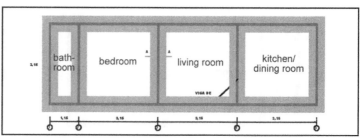

Typical foundation: floor plan

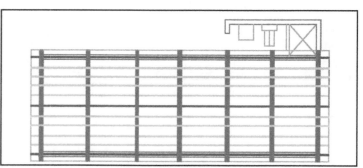

Details of a typical roof

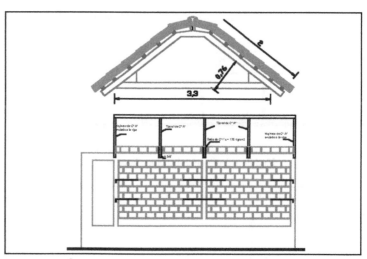

Structure of the cement block wall and saddle roof

Annex 3.1 Comparative analysis of the construction components implemented by Practical Action

QUINCHA

In San Martin, the process began with the evaluation of the materials available in the immediate or surrounding areas. Then the required aggregates were collected by mixed groups of men and women: stones, concrete and sand from the

QUINCHA MEJORADA: MADERA ROLLIZA   MADERA   CAÑA O CARRIZO

river banks (in the higher jungle). Groups were formed to transport the straw, cane, timber and wooden posts (shaina), using carriages or horses. The mud with straw or sawdust for the mud covering was prepared in an area adjacent or close to each plot.

The plot was levelled and cleared, then the layout of the house was drawn in accordance with the dimensions on the plan; 0.30m deep ditches were excavated for the walls and 0.70m ditches for the supporting wooden columns, the anchor blocks were 0.50m x 0.50m x 0.40m high. On top of these is placed a 0.30m x 0.30m x 0.12m foundation.

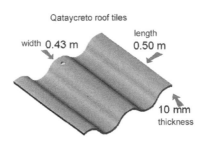

Qataycreto roof tiles
width 0.43 m   length 0.50 m
10 mm thickness

The parts of the supporting columns in contact with the soil were first protected with tar or oil and a ridge was made at the top as a support. Once the supporting columns were levelled and fitted, the concrete foundation was laid (cement = 1 bag of concrete = 18 'tins', 6mm stones (pebbles), a maximum of 30% of the total volume). Once the concrete has set, the main beams and roof beams were fitted and the wooden roof was completed and covered with the roof tiles that were called 'Qataycreto'.

To protect the walls, ditch reed and strips of pona (local palm) were used. The proportion of the mud placed over this cane was 6:1 earth and straw. The walls were left to dry for 15 days and then whitewashed.

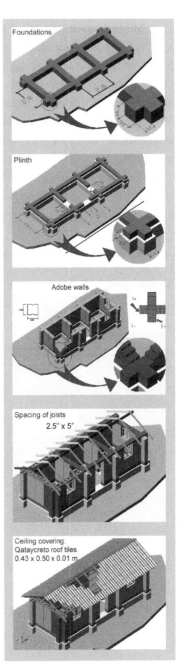

Foundations

Plinth

Adobe walls

Spacing of joists 2.5" x 5"

Ceiling covering: Qataycreto roof tiles 0.43 x 0.50 x 0.01 m

IMPROVED ADOBE

The walls built with improved adobe (0.38m x 0.38m x 0.12m), were reinforced with cross beams (beam unions), and cane reinforcements placed crosswise and upright, with a wooden ring beam on the top.

In Ayacucho, adobes can still be made as farm soil is abundant (this being a farming area). However, large areas are required to dry the adobes, which are not available in the town. Therefore, the adobes had to be dried in rather distant areas and then transported back, which increased the work. The straw for the adobes was collected in nearby hills by the beneficiaries, who also provided the eucalyptus wood for the roof of their homes (local manpower was hired to prepare this wood).

The work in this area was carried out after the rainy season. It is advisable to take the local climate into consideration when planning to implement projects.

In Moquegua, on the other hand, the initial technical proposal was to build with improved adobes; however, the implementation of the project was limited by significant factors: the shortage and poor quality of the land and the difficulty in obtaining dirt and cane for making the adobes in urban areas. In addition, in the extremely poor areas affected by the earthquake, the rugged topography and the small size of the plots made it difficult to build with adobe, as there was not enough space available to make it. Furthermore, the thickness of adobe walls significantly reduced the useful space available for the house. As a result of this experience, it was decided to change the technology for the next project and work with cement blocks.

For the roof structures in the Moquegua I project, the beams and cross bars were made of tornillo wood by a private company. Subsequently, the wooden pieces were transported and assembled in the housing project. The doors and windows were made by a small local businessman.

Graphic designs: Practical Action.

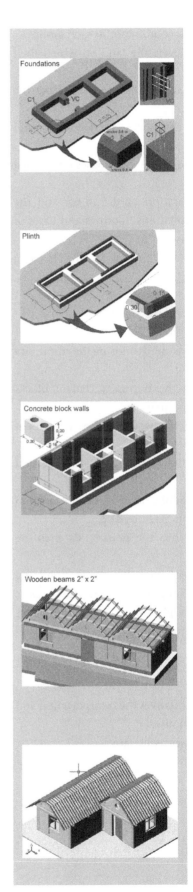

Foundations

Plinth

Concrete block walls

Wooden beams 2" x 2"

CONCRETE BLOCKS

This system was applied in the Moquegua II (Chen Chén) and La Yarada projects in Tacna, where the soil is sandy. Besides, concrete blocks were already produced in Tacna for construction purposes.

The specialized training provided in the workshop focused on improving the production of cement blocks, roof tiles and concrete beams and saddle roofs.

The equipment required to make the cement blocks were a vibrating machine, a mixer and six moulds, plus electricity to make them work. A team of six people was in charge of producing an average of 1,000 blocks a day: two for collecting the ingredients and preparing the mix, two to operate the machinery and two to transport the blocks to the drying area.

Every day, one person had to sprinkle them with water so that they would set.

Likewise, a team of six people was required to make the concrete saddle roofs and the covers for septic tanks.

To optimize the production of the components, a team was trained to specialize in cutting and bending the iron bars for the cross frames, foundation beams, columns and for building the standard structures in accordance with the module.

Another temporary workshop was held to make the micro-concrete roof tiles referred to as 'Qataycreto', to which end a flat concrete surface was required, a water tank was built for the setting process, an average of five vibrating machines were used, and wooden platforms for drying the tiles.

Tests were carried out to control the weight.

Sanitary matrices were also made for the water and sewage networks. In addition, a wood or metal carpentry workshop was implemented on site for the manufacture of wooden or metal matrices, wooden doors and wooden or metal window frames were made by a small local entrepreneur.

In general, the entire work process and the role of each participant in obtaining the housing components were explained and when they should join the groups to make the components. The benefits of 'teamwork' were justified and participants were told how they should organize themselves in accordance with their skills, preferences or personal needs.

The experience was dynamic and adaptable: the methodologies were modified to improve team performances and the quality of the components was monitored. Men and women participated, working more than 10 hours a day.

Construction process:

1. Establish a schedule for the construction work and for coordination meetings.

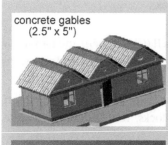

concrete gables
(2.5" x 5")

2. Form four teams and appoint a team coordinator in each group.

3. The beneficiary family clears and levels the land on which their house will be built.

4. A construction technician and a team of three people lay out the land in accordance with the plans.

5. The concrete, stones and other aggregates are identified and selected.

6. The cement and iron are transported to the warehouses established by the committee.

7. Training is provided on the preparation of the mixes and the proportion of materials for the foundations, footings and bases of the walls, in one of the selected houses.

8. Transportation of the aggregates and timber for the housing foundations.

9. Digging the pits.

10. Fitting the foundation beam and columns (concrete).

11. Laying the cement and footings, in groups.

12. The organisation of the groups is monitored to ensure the continuity of and participation in the work.

13. Distribution and transportation of the necessary cement blocks from the production area to the respective site.

14. Training on settling and building the walls (adobes or cement blocks).

15. Training on column forming for the beneficiaries who are best qualified for construction work.

16. Making the wooden ring beam for adobe housing, or forming and filling the concrete ring beam for concrete housing.

17. Fitting the concrete saddle roofs onto the houses. Six men are required to lift each one.

18. Building the roof and fitting the roof tiles: this involves building the standard wooden structure to support the tiles. This work is carried out by a trainer and three people, lining up the four points of each section and evenly distributing the wooden bars, approximately every 50cm.

19. The tiles are tied onto the wooden bar with wire, working from the bottom towards the top of the roof.

20. Water and sewage installations: this involves the transportation and installation of the matrices in each house.

21. The beneficiaries each build their own septic tanks.

22. The concrete floors are laid and polished.

23. Doors and windows are fitted.

24. Inside and outside walls are plastered.

25. Walls are painted.

Graphic designs: Practical Action.

Annex 4.1 Training workshops on construction technologies

This annex also includes the records of the workshops held with project beneficiaries to design their future housing, particularly in Alto Mayo (San Martin), where the participation was greater and there was more time to implement them.

It also contains a description of the experience in the workshops to manufacture the construction components, which were held at the same time as the demolitions or on site layouts of the new houses. These workshops, which were held for different teams led by members of the population with the expert advice of Practical Action technicians, also focused on the organization and participation of the different agents involved.

The records also describe the technology employed for manufacturing the construction components, as well as the systems and techniques for building with improved 'quincha', adobe walls, concrete blocks and 'Qataycreto' roof tiles. The technical housing construction processes are also explained.

Once the beneficiaries had moved into their homes, they developed some improvements for their own particular comfort, as a result of the construction skills they learnt and, in other cases, using their creativity within their limited budgets. It would be interesting to consider these contributions and improvements to the initial design for future housing designs in areas with a similar climate and similar cultural characteristics.

Practical Action – CONSTRUCTION WORKSHOPS
ALTO MAYO, AYACUCHO, MOQUEGUA and TACNA

Design workshops

The design workshops were held in two sessions with the project's beneficiary families. The characteristics of their previous houses were considered and improvements were proposed by Practical Action.

In Alto Mayo the group was encouraged to base their work on their own lifestyle and participate in the design of their house bearing in mind the spaces required by family members. With this guidance, they were able to draw sketches of their future homes. Subsequently, small blocks of wood of different colours were used so that they could identify each area of the house and thus obtain a clearer idea of the whole house, which could cover an area of approximately 30m^2.

In Ayacucho, Moquegua and Tacna, models obtained from the previous research work described in previous pages were used and lineal rooms were generally defined. In Chen Chén and La Yarada, the families required two rooms: a bedroom and a living room, providing they did not already have a house in the first place.

Construction training workshops

The training consisted of different methodologies based on the local cultural characteristics and the construction technology in each area of involvement. Basically, construction workshops were held applying a demonstration technology, to which end scale models of improved construction systems on a scale of 1:1 were produced and this technique was applied to the construction of community buildings initially, and subsequently to housing construction.

Since the objective was to use local natural resources, the beneficiaries were expected to contribute timber, earth, sand, gravel and straw.

In Ayacucho, Moquegua and Tacna, the workshop methodology recovered the population's community work methods referred to as 'aini' and 'minka', reciprocal work inherited from pre-Inca times which continues to this day.

Technical assistance for self-construction

Each project had an average of four technicians. Three of them worked on construction aspects and one trained people to make and fit roof tiles. Each project also required local staff who were trained by Practical Action and referred to as 'extension workers', consisting of three men and three women who took on different roles during the implementation of the project.

In Alto Mayo, the promotion and training work on construction systems was carried out by technical staff trained by Practical Action. Both the training staff and the trainees replicated their experience in reconstruction projects implemented by various institutions over the last 15 years.

The know-how and experience transferred to the project beneficiaries by construction foremen, technicians and 'extension workers', required theoretical and practical training at the same time.

Organization of the beneficiaries

Organization skills were improved for both teamwork and individual work. Groups of ten people were formed, as this was considered an adequate number for distributing tasks. It was evident that some families wanted to carry out the construction work individually, due to their personal differences with other beneficiaries.

The following activities were carried out:

Group activities

1. Carrying aggregates, manufacturing and producing construction components.
2. Construction: building walls
3. Roofing

Individual work

1. Whitewashing walls
2. Floors

Photographs: Practical Action.

Practical Action – TALLERES
ALTO MAYO, AYACUCHO, MOQUEGUA and TACNA

Design workshops

Workshop in Alto Mayo

Alto Mayo: technical supervision

Alto Mayo: individual work

Practical Action – WORKSHOPS
ALTO MAYO, AYACUCHO, MOQUEGUA and TACNA

General view of the workshop: Moquegua

Producing roof tiles and bending iron

Women participants

Children cooperate and learn

Workshop in the Chen Chén plains

Photographs by the authors

Practical Action-CONSTRUCTION WORKSHOPS
ALTO MAYO, AYACUCHO, MOQUEGUA and TACNA

In Moquegua and Tacna, the component manufacturing workshops were held due to the need to manufacture cement blocks, roof trusses and roof tiles. To this end, appropriate land was required. In Chen Chén, free areas were used; in Tacna, the National Police provided their premises to store the materials and tools and the Irrigation Committee provided some of the necessary tools.

Administration of resources
This consisted of the delivery of construction materials to each of the beneficiaries, keeping records of incoming and outgoing materials. This improved people's commitment and the progress of the works.

Levels of specialization
The group construction process was defined by the participants themselves and the roofing stages were established by each family.

Teams were formed and the work was speeded up with an organized production of the necessary construction components. The participation in specialization workshops was based on the capacity, gender and age of the people. The men carried out activities that required physical strength and their technical reasoning skills were applied to the layout and construction of the walls and the forming and assembly of the roofs.

Participation of the women, the elderly and children
The participation of women and children was very significant. Some of them revealed great talent for construction work even though they had never participated before, because traditionally these are considered exclusively men's tasks.

The tasks they did best were those that required rhythm and production in series, like moulding materials, preparing iron for the columns, walls and roofs, nailing things together, preparing cane for the 'quincha' walls, among others. Their physical constitution prevented them from carrying out activities that required great strength, like building with adobe bricks or cement blocks or lifting the roof trusses. 'Even among the couples involved, the women were the main participants in the reconstruction of their homes, either because their husbands were more involved in their farming chores or because the women felt a greater need to decide what to do with their homes' (Practical Action, no date).

Another outstanding aspect of the women's participation was their leadership of neighbourhood groups. 'For women with leadership skills, the experience of participating in these groups gave them the opportunity to discover or develop those skills, to the extent that they gradually took on internal organization tasks and negotiated with aid entities (Practical Action, no date).

Elderly people and children participated in the selection of material and in sifting and accumulating them; children between 12 and 15 years of age revealed similar skills to those of older women. In Moquegua, one 15 year-old built a house for his mother, who depended on him both physically and emotionally. When he was interviewed, he had taken on the role of head of household, taking the decision to stay in the same area and carry out the tasks that his mother no longer had the strength for. In the workshops, 14 and 15 year old children learnt to prepare iron and the younger children helped carry water and aggregates. These tasks helped them value the work carried out and their future home.

Assistance and integration
For women with small children who were working on the project on a daily basis, a provisional room was prepared where the mothers could feed their children and the children could play while their mothers worked.

On Sundays, sporting events were held between beneficiaries and the technical team of Practical Action, to strengthen the ties and communication between them.

CONTRIBUTIONS OF BENEFICIARIES

In Chuschi, Ayacucho, some beneficiaries improved the final design of their homes, such as putting a drain pipe on the roof and a wide path leading to the house, thus preventing water from entering the house during the rainy season.

During the rainy season, they found it necessary to incorporate rain drains and put in improvised ceilings. This proved that there is a need that was not anticipated in the design, which should be considered in the future. In Moquegua, a patio was added to the L-shaped module, formed by the two walls of the module and a fence with a straw matting roof and a polished cement floor. With a small investment, an additional useful area was added to the housing module, which was very appropriate for the hot and dry climate in Moquegua.

The initiative to incorporate front gardens in the newly completed homes created a homely atmosphere, adding comfort to the reconstruction conditions of the Machu Picchu association.

The beneficiaries used their own imagination to crown the facades of their homes, thus confirming their sense of identification with their house.

Photographs: the authors

Bibliography

AZABACHE, D. (2003) 'Final reports from the Chuschi, Moquegua and Tacna projects' Practical Action, Lima.

BERNAL ESQUIA, I. (2000) 'Seismicity characteristics of the southern region of Peru', Research Journal, Lima. National Centre of Geographic Data – The Geophysical Institute of Peru.

CHACALTANA, J. (2004) 'Can poverty be prevented in Peru?', Lima, CIES(Consortium of Economic and Social Investigation).

CHUQUISENGO, O. and GAMARRA, L. (2001) 'Proposed methodology for local risk and disaster management, a practical study'. Practical Action, Manos Unidas.

International Red Cross and Red Crescent Movement (2003) 'International report on disasters'.

FERRADAS, P. (2000) 'Water from the sky and earth, impact of the El Nino phenomenon in Peru. Local perspectives and experiences, Lima', Predes, Diakonia.

FERRADAS, P. and MEDINA, N. (2003) 'Disaster risks and children's rights', Lima, Practical Action, Save the Children.

GIESECKE, A. and ZEGARRA, L. (1997) 'Reinforcement of existing adobe housing' Lima, Project Ceresis-GTZ-PUCP.

Practical Action Peru–Cáritas del Peru (1995) Alto Mayo. The reconstruction of a village, Lima, Practical Action.

KUROIWA, J. (2004) 'Disaster prevention. Living in harmony with nature', Lima, Editorial Bruño.

LAVELL, A., editor, (1994) 'To the north of Río Grande – social sciences and disasters, a North American perspective.' Bogota, La Red-Practical Action.

MARUSSI CASTELLÁN, F. (1989) 'Historical background of quincha', Ininvi.

MASKREY, A., editor, (1996) 'Earthquakes in the humid tropics' Bogota, La Red-Practical Action.

MEDINA, J. (1991) 'Geodynamic phenomena – Study and treatment measures'. Lima, Practical Action Peru.

MONZÓN, F. and OLIDEN, J. (1990) 'Technology and popular housing'. Lima, Practical Action.

MONZÓN, F. (1994) 'Final report from the Alto Mayo project', Practical Action (photocopy).

PREDES – CIED (1984) 'Landslides and flooding in the Rimac Valley', Lima, PREDES CIED.

PRACTICAL ACTION (no date) 'Reconstruction and development of Alto Mayo, Peru', final report, Lima.

PREDES (2002) 'Construction with improved quincha. Guide to the self-construction of housing', Lima, PREDES.

SENCICO (1995) 'Prefabricated quincha. Manufacture and Construction'.

SENCICO Research and Standardization Management (2001) Concrete blocks – manufacture and construction. Second edition. Lima, SENCICO.

SENCICO –Materials Bank (2001) 'Improved adobe houses'. (Primer). Lima, SENCICO.

SILGADO, Enrique. (1998) History of Peru's strongest earthquakes (1513–1974). Lima, Ingeomin (now Ingemmet).

TEJADA, Urbano (2001) Good land – Notes for adobe designs and constructions. Lima, CIDAP.

VARGAS, Julio and Daniel TORREALVA (1986) 'Dissemination of the adobe technology in a housing reconstruction project.' Lima, PUCP–AID.